How to Proofread Your Own Writing

Tips and Techniques to Help You Produce an Error-Free Manuscript

SANDIE GILES

Copyright © 2013 Sandie Giles

ISBN: 1484179587

ISBN-13: 978-1484179581

CONTENTS

INTRODUCTION

Today, with the proliferation of mobile phones enabling us not only to talk to other people while on the move, but to send eMails, texts and to update our social networks, we tend to communicate more by the written than by the spoken word. The fast pace of these communications means that we have become so accustomed to text speak and one hundred and forty character messages, using questionable abbreviations, that you might imagine correct spelling, grammar and punctuation were things of the past. If you want to be taken seriously as a writer, they most certainly are not. Unfortunately, many people either don't believe this to be true or are in complete denial about it.

The advent of easy-to-access and virtually cost-free self-publishing platforms has meant that many of these same people are jumping into the fray without any knowledge of the book publishing industry or the processes involved in publishing a book.

It is a recipe for disaster.

I'm hoping that the reason you've bought this book is because you're not one of those people. You know that you need to take the production of your book seriously and you realise that, if you don't, you will almost certainly receive negative reviews of your work that have nothing to do with the story you have written or the information you are trying to impart. If so, you are already one step ahead of the masses.

There is no doubt in my mind that employing a professional to proofread your book is the best option, but I know that many people will not even consider this option or have severe doubts about the benefits of doing so. Therefore, my aim is to give you all the information you need on the proofreading process to make a reasoned decision as to whether you should proceed on your own, or not. In the end, only you can make that decision, but if you are going to proofread your own book, then at least you will be armed with the knowledge to do the best possible job you can.

DON'T DO IT

Not everyone is suited to proofreading. That is a simple fact that you will have to accept. You might not have the skill or the patience required. You might not have enough time to dedicate to the process. I can't tell you whether it is right or wrong for you, but I can tell you the types of people I think should not even consider it.

Bad at Spelling and Grammar

You have to be realistic about your own abilities. If you're bad at spelling and grammar, it is unlikely that you are ever going to be able to proofread your manuscript effectively, because you won't be able to see your own mistakes. Be honest with yourself and you will know whether or not you should proceed.

It Doesn't Matter – My Story Will Shine Through

If you really do believe that, then I'm not sure why you're reading this book, but I can tell you, without any shadow of a doubt, that you are wrong.

If you think you'll be able to get by without taking into account any of the rules and all you are prepared to do is give your manuscript a cursory glance for any glaring spelling errors, you will soon find out that people don't want to read your book.

Non-Native Speaker

First, let me say that this is not a comment on non-native speakers writing books in English. I think it's amazing that you're able to do so – I certainly wouldn't even contemplate writing in another language.

However, I have read many samples of self-published books that haven't been edited or proofread, and it is always obvious when they are by non-native English speakers. This is because the language used is often too formal, the phrasing isn't natural and sometimes the words chosen are used incorrectly.

This kind of writing will jar with a native speaker and they probably won't get past the preview to buy your book. Why take the risk of getting it wrong? Please, get a native English speaker to edit and proofread your work for you.

Not Good at Formatting

At this stage you're probably wondering why I've included this category here. It's because proofreading is not just about making sure the words on the page are correct. It's about ensuring the presentation is perfect as well.

If you don't know how to indent your text or create paragraph spacing, then you need to get someone to do this for you because, as with the case of people who are not good at spelling, it is highly likely that you won't be able to see where your errors are, and even if you do, you won't know how to solve them.

By all means, check the text yourself, but get an experienced person to help you with the formatting.

***

Even if you are competent at spelling, punctuation, grammar and formatting, it is possible that after reading this book you will feel that you cannot possibly spend the time required to proofread your manuscript properly. In this case, I would strongly advise you to get a professional to do th ɔ for you.

THIS BOOK'S FOCUS

This book is primarily aimed at those who want to self-publish, although the techniques and tips discussed can be used to proofread any type of document (eg, presentations, job applications, dissertations or even your own website).

(NB: *This book is not a tutorial on how to become a professional proofreader.*)

Even if you are writing a book and are not intending to self-publish, but to submit your manuscript to an agent or publisher, you should also consider using these techniques. A manuscript that is well-presented and has very few errors will create a far better impression on the recipient. Publishers and agents want authors who are prepared to put in the work to make their manuscript as good as it can be, even before they have seen it, and if you can prove that you have, that's one less reason for them to reject you.

HOW WILL WE TACKLE THIS TASK?

First, I will discuss the role of a professional proofreader and how you can relate that to your own manuscript. Then, I will outline the common types of errors that get missed and how you can try to avoid them and finally, I will talk about formatting and how you should prepare your manuscript for eReader conversion and Print-on-Demand (POD), with an emphasis on correct formatting conventions, readability and the additional proofreading challenges that entails.

(NB: *Where specific word processing functions are mentioned in the text, they will refer to the functions found in Microsoft Word for PC.*)

CAN I REALLY DO THIS MYSELF?

I believe that, with a good deal of care and attention, it is possible to effectively proofread your own manuscript, but it takes time and dedication. You need to weigh that up against the cost of paying someone to do it for you. When you have finished reading this book, you will be in a position to judge whether producing a high quality book is a viable proposition for you.

And in case you're wondering, this book has been created without the help of any outside professional services, ie, I produced it entirely on my own. It wouldn't have been fair to have done otherwise, would it? It will give you a real example of what can be achieved.

Could it have been better if I had used professional help? Well, I'll leave that question for later.

CHOICES

Anyone who publishes a book has to choose a style of writing that they are comfortable with. Styles change a lot over time. Many of the books that are considered classics from one hundred years ago, or more, are littered with adjectives, adverbs and run-on sentences. No-one thought that was wrong back then. They most certainly do now.

What's my style? Well, you'll no doubt already have realised, I am British. Therefore, I will be using British English spellings and terminology. I prefer my writing to be informal, so you will find sentences starting with 'And', 'Or' and 'But'. I make no apologies for that. It is quite deliberate.

With regard to the text, I have had to make choices about words where there is more than one spelling or format. I know that some of you will already be querying the spelling I have used for proofreading. Shouldn't it be proof reading? Or even proof-reading? All three variations exist in common usage. I decided to go with the one in my dictionary. You may use whichever form you prefer for this and any other word with multiple forms – as long as you're consistent.

TECHNICAL TERMS

I've already mentioned that when I refer to formatting functions, I'm discussing the use of Microsoft Word for PC. In order to make it clear that I am talking about a Microsoft Word function, these terms will be capitalised. I will also use word processing terms in preference to proofreading terms in most instances, as these are more likely to be understood by those without previous proofreading experience.

UNDERSTANDING PROOFREADING

The first thing you need to know is that proofreading is extremely difficult.

There, I've said it.

I don't want anyone reading this book to be under the illusion that proof-reading your own manuscript is easy. It isn't. Proofreading, carried out properly, is a painstaking and time-consuming process. In addition, for those without meticulous minds and the patience of a saint, it is not necessarily an enjoyable task.

But it has to be done. If it isn't, your book reviews will focus more on your spelling and grammar than the story (or advice) you have written – and none of us wants that to happen.

So, what makes proofreading your own words so difficult? Let's take an example of something much shorter than your manuscript to start with. Does this sound familiar?

You carefully read through an eMail you're about to send, or a status update for your social media page that you want to post, to check that everything is correct and then, only once you've pressed send or post, do you see that one glaring error that will make everyone who reads it think you're an illit-erate idiot. Well, they probably won't think that, but that's your gut reaction as you ram your forehead with the heel of your palm.

We all have the tendency to gloss over this type of error when we're checking text because we're so eager to get the thing sent. The key is not to rush. What we really should do is leave it for five or ten minutes and go back and read it again before pressing send, but we don't.

So, impatience is the first factor that leads to bad proofreading.

The second is familiarity.

I want you to think about your manuscript now. How many times have you read through it by the time you get to the proofreading stage? Two? Ten? Twenty? More?

All those rounds of drafts and edits that have taken weeks, months, or years to achieve, take their toll. When you know a text that well, it isn't surprising that your eyes will gloss over even obvious errors without realising it.

This is not your fault, and it's one of the reasons why the fresh eyes of a professional proofreader are a good idea if you can afford it, but there are many steps you can take to help yourself with the process.

A DEFINITION

Before we start discussing techniques, we need to define, and understand, what proofreading actually entails.

Many people get confused about the difference between proofreading and editing, or think that proofreading is the equivalent of a simple spell check or grammar check of their manuscript, by their computer, once everything else is completed. We need to clear up those misunderstandings now.

The dictionary definition for proofreading, as provided by my electronic Collins Dictionary, is:

> *"To read copy (or printer's proofs) to detect and mark errors to be corrected."*

And the definition for editing is:

> *"To prepare (text) for publication by checking and improving its accuracy, clarity, etc."*

That's all very well in simple terms, but it doesn't really tell you very much. There is some overlap between the two roles, as these definitions suggest, but their primary focus is different, as is the time at which they are performed in the publishing process.

Editing is always carried out before proofreading and, in traditional publishing, is carried out before the book is typeset. Proofreading is always carried out after typesetting, ie, the book is already in draft book format (although not yet bound).

There are different kinds of editors, but in generalised terms, an editor will look for errors in grammar, spelling and punctuation as they read through the manuscript, but they will also look for issues with the style of writing and the structure of the book. So, they might decide whether or not the manuscript is written in a suitable way for the market it is aimed at, or they might highlight issues with plot (plot holes and inconsistencies, for example). They are looking to improve the text and the story to make it right for the market.

A proofreader will take the draft book and mark errors. These may be errors with the initial manuscript that weren't spotted by the editor, or errors that have been introduced in the typesetting process. They will check that corrections made by the editor have been implemented and that the formatting corresponds to the correct house style. Proofreading is the final checking stage of the publishing process and may be performed more than once, and by more than one person.

In the self-publishing process, the workflow should follow a similar order, even though you might be doing most of the work yourself.

The manuscript should be edited (which should catch initial proofreading errors), it should then be formatted for the publishing platform (the equivalent of typesetting) and finally, the proofreading should be carried out on the POD- or eBook-ready version (before and after actual conversion).

It is extremely important that all editing is carried out before the proofreading stage. Otherwise, you might introduce further errors when editing the text that never get proofread.

THE ROLE

Exactly what kind of errors does a professional proofreader look for? Let's delve into that in a little more detail.

When you employ a proofreader to correct your manuscript, they should be looking for some, or all of the following, depending on what has been agreed in your contract:

Spelling Errors and Typos

What does everyone immediately think of when proofreading is mentioned? Spelling errors and typos. Of course, a proofreader will look for these, but they are only a very small part of the remit.

Misused Words

You might think that this comes under spelling errors, but what we're talking about here is, for example, two words that sound the same but are spelled differently (and have different meanings). The subtle difference requires a slightly different mindset when reading a manuscript.

Missing and Extra Words

This kind of error often happens during the editing process, when the text hasn't been read through again afterwards with fresh eyes. You might have left half of an old sentence in because you didn't highlight it properly, for example, or not have added all the words necessary to make a phrase work.

Repeated Words

This is when the same significant word (or phrase) is used several times within the space of a few sentences. The proofreader will suggest an appropriate alternative.

Punctuation Errors

Punctuation is probably the second thing most people think of if pushed to describe the role of a proofreader. It is incredibly easy for a comma to slip in where a full stop should be or for text to be incorrectly punctuated, especially in regards to speech and the often dreaded apostrophe.

Text Indentation

There are certain rules for text indentation and paragraph styles that have to be followed and these will be checked according to house style for the publisher.

Incorrect End-of-Line Hyphenation

Typesetting software automatically hyphenates words at the ends of lines and, although the software works extremely well most of the time, there are instances where the proofreader has to overrule its decisions. For example, words may have been broken in a place that could be misleading to the reader.

Spacing

It is very easy to insert extra spaces between sentences (especially for those of us who were taught to type on a typewriter), between words, or to have an extra line space between paragraphs or sections. Spotting these can be very difficult and it takes a keen eye to get it right.

Widows and Orphans

Widows and orphans are single lines of paragraphs at the bottom or top of a page. These are easy to spot, but may take a bit of work to eliminate.

Headings

Headings are checked for the correct font style and font size, as well as for consistency across chapters and sections. This is usually done in a completely separate pass, as it is much easier to spot the errors this way.

Footnotes and Endnotes

It is important that all footnotes and endnotes are correctly referenced and placed in the text, otherwise the reader may be directed to incorrect (and confusing) information.

Graphics

Graphics are checked for correct placement, captioning and numbering, as well as for their content.

Consistency

Everything is checked for consistency. In addition to all those elements already mentioned, this means checking that names don't change halfway through the text, that spelling is consistent (eg, -ise or -ize spelling), or that capitalisation is consistent, etc.

***

This list gives you an overview of the role, but I have only included the things that are likely to be relevant to a self-publisher (each of these tasks will be explained in further detail later in the book). There are many additional proofreading tasks carried out for a traditionally published book, but even so, I think you'll agree there are a lot of things to consider, especially when you have to do it for yourself.

Do you always check your manuscript for *all* of these things? I'm guessing not, but that's probably one of the reasons you're reading this book – to find out what you need to do.

As you can see, proofreading is complex and cannot be completed successfully by a simple read through of your manuscript on the screen.

START PLANNING NOW

No proofreader can start a job without a style sheet and neither should you. A style sheet is a document that contains all the specifications for the job you are working on. It includes such things as:

- Font style and font size for main text;
- Heading styles, including alignment, font style and size, emboldening or italics and space (line space) from the text above and below;
- British or American spelling;
- -ize or -ise spelling;
- A list of technical words, or specific spelling choices, listed alphabetically (this could include character names in a novel) and which words should always be hyphenated;
- The style for the book (eg, chatty or formal);
- House style for punctuation (eg, single or double quotes);
- How running headers should be set (eg, left-aligned, right-aligned, font, font size);

- How graphics should be displayed (eg, centred, wrapped text, numbering);
- How footnotes and endnotes should appear.

The list goes on and on. Don't worry if you don't understand what some of these mean. They'll all be explained later.

You need to create a style sheet for yourself. It doesn't need to be as detailed as it would be for a proofreader working for a publishing house, but it should include the basics of your format, style and spelling for your book.

Why not keep a sheet of paper and a pen beside you as you read so that you can make notes on things to include in your own style sheet? You might not have already made all the decisions necessary for formats, etc, but it will remind you that those decisions need to be made before you begin proofreading.

ERRORS WILL SLIP THROUGH

There's something else you should know before you begin.

However hard you try, and however careful you are, you will have to accept that no published book is ever one hundred per cent error-free. Even traditionally published books have errors in them, especially the digital editions, and they often won't get corrected until a second edition is published, if at all. The only time they are likely to be corrected immediately is if they could be misleading or dangerous (such as in a manual) or if they appear in a children's book.

I hate making errors, but I can guarantee you that there is at least one glaring error in this book. Yes, a book about proofreading – and I don't mean the deliberate errors in the examples. But, if you do find an error, please bear with me until the end when you will be able to fully appreciate the difficulties of the task.

Above all, don't rush your proofreading and do the best job you possibly can.

And don't forget – you have one huge advantage over traditional publishing. As a self-publisher, you have the opportunity to correct errors and upload a new file as soon as you discover them and you should take full advantage of this facility.

PRELIMINARY TECHNIQUES

First of all, what do I mean by preliminary techniques?

To my mind, there is only one true method of proofreading and that is to print out your manuscript and go through it line-by-line. However, there are many other techniques you can use before getting to that stage (you could use them while editing, for example).

Some are good for picking up spelling errors, others for noticing missing words. Few are good for punctuation errors, other than when you run out of breath when reading because of a lack of commas.

There are some listed here that I would never use myself, but I know that some people swear by them and it would be unfair of me to miss them out. There is even one that I think could be detrimental to your book (you won't be in any doubt about which one that is), but I have included it so that I could explain why I think that.

Use as many of them as you find helpful – the more the better – apart from the first one listed. That one, I strongly recommend to everyone.

WAIT

Remember those two things I mentioned back at the beginning that are extremely detrimental to your ability to proofread – impatience and familiarity? Well, you're going to have to quash your feelings of impatience to rid yourself of familiarity and practise the art of waiting.

Waiting might seem like an odd thing to categorise as a technique, but I really believe it is one of the best things you can do to improve the effectiveness of your proofreading.

Putting your manuscript away and ignoring it for a period of time means that when you come to proofread, you will be less familiar with the text. Okay, no-one is going to claim that you'll have forgotten every single word, but you will have blurred the memory of how each sentence is constructed, which will make it easier for you to pick out any errors.

How long should you wait?

The easy answer to that question is to wait as long as possible – only the waiting really isn't that easy. You will be dying to get on with finalising the text and the thought of squirreling the document away in a drawer (real or electronic) for even a couple of days can be unbearable. Believe me. I know.

Resist the urge to touch that manuscript. It will be worth it. I promise.

Ideally, you should leave your manuscript for a couple of months. Alternatively, leave it for at least one week (I mean it), or as long after that as you can manage.

You're still not convinced that you should wait? Let me try to prove it to you.

The Value of Waiting

I want you to look at the following sentence and tell me how many errors you can see in the text.

the q u i c k brown fox jumped over the lazy dog

Are you done? How many mistakes did you find? One? Two? Three?

I'm hoping you noticed that there was no capital letter at the beginning of the sentence and, of course, you noticed the missing full stop at the end. Good. How about the extra spacing that seems to have worked its way into the word quick? You didn't see that? You might have thought it was a glitch in the printing, if you noticed it at all.

Okay, that final one may have been a little unfair – you weren't expecting that kind of error and it would be unusual for it to happen in a word processing document.

Let's try another.

She sell seashells in the sea shore.

That one was easy, wasn't it? The missing 's' on sells. 'In' instead of 'on'. What about sea shore? Shouldn't that be one word? Because of the way you say this rhyme in your head, seashore sounds like two words – each exists in its own right, after all – so, it's very easy to miss and it is something for which your spell checker will be of no help at all.

We all make similar mistakes to this when we're typing. You can be the best speller in the world, but if your fingers and your brain aren't working at the same speed, what comes out will be less than perfect. How many times have you typed 'your' instead of 'you're' and when you go back and read the text you chastise yourself, because you know the difference?

The reason I used these two pieces of text is because they are so familiar to all of us. We know them off by heart. We've been hearing them since we were kids and, for some of us, that's a long time. Therefore, when we read them, we gloss over what we are reading without even realising it. This is exactly what will happen if you don't let your manuscript wait in that (virtual) drawer and you won't be able to do anything about it.

Still not sure I'm telling the truth? Let's examine a little further how your brain can fill in the gaps without you realising it.

You're on social media, right? You have to be – you're a writer.

You've probably seen one of those pictures posted where at the bottom it says 'you misread that' and you do a double-take, re-read it and find that you did misread it and you think how stupid you were. You were concentrating on the cute, or controversial, picture that was underneath the words, so your brain simply filled in what it thought it should see.

Or, you might have seen one of those pieces of text where all the letters in the words are jumbled, and you know that they're jumbled, but you can still understand them. In fcat, the txet can be a cmoplete mses nad you cna sitll raed it wouthit a pobelrm.

And then there are the the ones where the

DAER EB NAC SDROW
ERA YEHT NEHW
LLEW SA SDRAWKCAB

Now, do you understand why you need to wait? Your brain is a wonderful thing, but its ability to fill in the gaps can be a real problem when you're proofreading.

Did you see the deliberate error in the text you've just read?

All that jumbled up text might have made you gloss over it, because you would never normally have let 'the the' pass you by. That's a glaring error by anyone's standards.

If you did see it – well done. If you didn't – don't be put off. I deliberately hid it in amongst text that I knew would take your mind off the game.

If you still can't see it, look just above the backwards text. Got it? Good.

GRAMMAR CHECKERS

I know plenty of people use these, otherwise they wouldn't exist, but do you really want a computer to correct your writing for you?

Before I discuss this option, I have to come clean and admit that I have never used a grammar checker to go through an entire document, although I have looked at the suggestions in Microsoft Word every now and then and I tested a paragraph of this book in two online checkers.

One highlighted four stylistic errors and one vocabulary error, but it wouldn't show me exactly what it had picked up without me signing up for a free trial of that particular product.

The other highlighted one word (presumably the vocabulary error the previous checker had picked up) and suggested an alternative, which was completely inappropriate in the context. Apparently, it wasn't in the least bit concerned about the style errors.

Merely noting that difference should make you wonder how effective they are, but let me explain further why I would not use this kind of software.

Have you ever used one of those online translators? There's a very easy one you can find on that most popular of search engines. Yes, you know the one. All you have to do is plug in your phrase and it will churn out a translation in your chosen language in a matter of seconds.

I used that translator to put in a very common, standard phrase in French that we all learned at school, to see how it would translate it into English:

"Comment vous-appellez-vous?"

We all know (or, at least, those of us who passed our French exams do) that the equivalent question in English is:

"What is your name?"

The translator gave me:

"How you call yourself?"

By any stretch of the imagination, that's a bad translation.

I also tried out the translation in the opposite direction, from English to French, and put in:

"What is your name?"

It was translated as:

"Quel est votre nom?"

Once again, this can be understood, but is not necessarily how a native would say it (or it may be that this is the correct form and we were all taught the wrong thing at school).

I know you're asking, 'Why am I talking about translators when we are concerned with grammar checking?', but please bear with me a little longer.

Think of the computer grammar checker as a computer trying to speak your language (which is effectively what it is trying to do) by using a set of pre-programmed rules. We all know that English is a difficult language to learn, so those rules are very complex. Why should a computer find it easy? We don't. In fact, if we all found it easy, we wouldn't ever need to check our own grammar, would we? The computer will make mistakes, just like we do, but we will wrongly assume that the computer is always right and, I think, that is where the danger lies in relying on this type of software.

You see, in most cases, the software is only suggesting a change, it is not telling you that what it is suggesting is correct. You still have to understand why it is highlighting a word or a phrase and you might have to look up the grammar point in order to make a decision as to whether or not you want to accept it. However, many people simply take the suggestion as being correct because they are under the false impression that computers are never wrong. And grammar checkers miss mistakes as well. Just because one didn't find any errors on a page, doesn't mean that there aren't any.

Finally, we all make stylistic choices when we write. As I highlighted earlier in this book, I often start sentences with 'And' or 'But'. This is, according to many grammar sources, incorrect, and a grammar checker would pull me up on it every time. However, this type of breaking the rules is very common in more informal writing styles. If I had to go through declining a change every time I deliberately broke the rules, it would drive me crazy. (NB: *I do realise that some of the more advanced grammar checkers have ways of eliminating picking up particular style issues, but they are likely to be the paid versions.*)

Having said all that, the choice is yours.

If you find a grammar checker you are confident is giving you reasonable suggestions and you understand why it is making those suggestions, then use it to help you, but please don't always click 'Accept' and don't use it as your only proofreading check.

ASK A FRIEND

We all have a friend who is a stickler for grammar and punctuation, don't we? If you know that you're not very good at finding errors in your own writing, you can use their expertise to help you with your manuscript – as long as they're willing, of course. The more sets of eyes that have looked over the text before finalising it, the better. However, there are some important points to consider before you go ahead and stretch your friendship to the limit.

- Are you absolutely certain this person is as good as you think they are? If they aren't, they could do more damage than good to your manuscript. Maybe you should ask them to look over a short story or a single chapter first and see what they highlight before committing to an eighty thousand word novel.

- Agree some kind of payment for their services. Someone who is receiving payment for a task is much more likely to perform it to a high standard, even if all you can offer is a bottle of wine or a burger before the football match.

- Define what you are expecting from them, ie, they are looking for errors in spelling, grammar, punctuation and formatting, not editing the content. If they start editing the content, and you accept their changes, you will need to start the proofreading process all over again.

- Get a commitment as to when you can expect to get the manuscript back. If this person has a full-time job, three children and lots of hobbies, it could take them a long time to finish. Be realistic about their ability to complete the task within a reasonable timeframe. (And remember, we all have a different definition of what is reasonable.)

- Make sure they know that you won't be offended if your manuscript comes back with red marks all over it and that you want them to highlight *all* the errors.

- Don't be offended if your manuscript does come back looking like the pages are bleeding. Let it sit for a couple of days until you have your emotions in check and read it with your sensible head on. And don't forget that you don't have to accept all the changes they've made.

- If you don't understand why they have changed something, ask them, or get your grammar book or dictionary out and look it up.

If you do decide to use a friend to help you, don't rely on them to have found everything. Use some of the other techniques listed here as well to really blitz your manuscript.

READ OUT LOUD

No, I'm not talking about an open mike night down at your local pub, or even in your front room with the eager faces of your family waiting to be enthralled. This type of reading out loud is, most definitely, a private affair.

Reading your manuscript out loud is a very good way of finding errors in the text that you might gloss over if you were reading it on the screen. When you are reading out loud, you have to focus more closely on the individual words and there is, what I will term, a stumble effect when something is wrong. This happens because the text doesn't flow properly, making it impossible to keep going. A stumble will *always* need to be rephrased or punctuated differently.

As you read, make any necessary changes on your computer. Then, re-read that sentence in its entirety before moving on.

If you really hate the sound of your own voice you might want to try using Text-to-Speech software (TTS). (See below.)

Although reading out loud is very good for finding spelling errors and misplaced words, I wouldn't recommend it for finding complex punctuation errors (such as ones related to dialogue). If you try reading the punctuation out loud, you will spoil the flow of the narrative and negate the benefits of this kind of exercise.

TEXT-TO-SPEECH SOFTWARE (TTS)

There is software available that you can use to read your text out to you, which you can find by an easy search on the internet using the 'text-to-speech' term. Other places you might find TTS software are on your eReader and in some versions of Microsoft Word.

I don't find this software very useful. In my experience, the voices are so unnatural that they distract from the content and that is of no use at all when trying to listen out for errors. All I can hear is the voice, not the words. It's possible that if I were to stick at it, I might get attuned to the voices, but I would rather simply read out loud myself.

However, everyone is different, and if you find it useful in helping you to spot errors, do add it to your preliminary proofreading tools.

READ BACKWARDS

This isn't a technique I use either, but I know that many people do use it and find it helpful. It is often quoted on forum posts as soon as someone mentions proofreading.

Reading your manuscript backwards detaches your mind from the flow of the text and makes you concentrate on the individual words. Therefore, it is a good technique for picking up misspellings, but is unlikely to highlight where you have used the wrong word or the wrong punctuation, because the way you are reading it won't give you the sense of the text.

Whilst writing this book, I experimented with using this technique on a section of text on the screen. It didn't work for me. I couldn't focus on the words properly. That may be just me – my eyesight or the particular glare on my screen. However, when I tried it on a print copy it worked well, but I did find my eyes wandering forwards a few words every now and then, which I found distracting, and I couldn't imagine using it for a whole book.

I don't think I'll be using it again, but the theory is sound if you want to try it out.

Some people also advocate reading the text upside down, which would have a similar effect.

CHANGE THE FORMAT

One technique that I find quite amazing, because you simply can't imagine that it would work, is changing the font of your manuscript (please make a copy first – you don't want to save your document in the other font by mistake and screw up all your formatting).

Just changing your Times New Roman to Arial will trick your brain into seeing the text with fresh eyes. Try it. Seriously, it does work. It also works if you simply save your document as a .pdf file because, even in the same font, it displays differently on the screen.

For example, this is what the previous paragraph looks like in Arial as opposed to Garamond (the font used for this print version):

Just by changing your Times New Roman to Arial will trick your brain into seeing the text with fresh eyes. Try it. Seriously, it does work. It also works if you simply save your document as a .pdf file because, even in the same font, it displays differently on the screen.

Also, if you have an eReader handy, there's nothing quite like seeing your manuscript as your potential reader will see it and looking at it on your eReader screen will have a similar effect on your brain to physically changing the font. It will also have the added advantage of highlighting other formatting errors.

PEN AND PAPER

Now, let's get down to the nitty-gritty of proofreading.

Your final stage of the process should always be to print out your manuscript so that you can read through the text in detail.

I know, I can hear you complaining now – that's a lot of paper and computer ink I'm going to waste. I do understand your concerns over the cost, but trying to spot all your errors on a computer screen is virtually impossible (it's difficult enough on paper) and it really isn't a waste of money, it's an investment. Your writing must be worth a tenner, surely?

If you need to be convinced further, here are some specific reasons why it is a bad idea to carry out your final proofread on a computer screen. Think for a moment about all the other things that sit there on your screen while you're working. They are all highly likely to distract your eyes and interrupt the task in hand:

- EMails pinging in the background or flashing in the corner;
- Social media updates that just have to be answered or commented upon right away;
- Adverts;
- The flashing cursor in your own document;
- The glare on your screen from the sunshine or the lamp behind you.

You can probably name many others. Anything that takes your attention away from the text could cause you to miss an error – and it only takes a second for that to happen.

In addition to the distractions, it is virtually impossible to read your text one line at a time when you are viewing it on a screen – your eyes will always see the other lines of text in your peripheral vision, making it impossible to fully focus on the line you are reading.

Proofreading a printed-out manuscript is essential and it is what we will now concentrate on.

THE TOOLKIT

You're ready to start. You have your manuscript printed out and in front of you, but what else do you need? My suggestions would be the following:

Ruler – A ruler (actually, you will need two rulers) will help you to read your text line-by-line by physically blocking out the line below. A solid colour or a wooden ruler is best, as a see-through one somewhat dilutes the effect.

Coloured Pen – A coloured pen should be used for marking corrections. Corrections marked in black are difficult to see against text printed in black. If you do use a black pen, you may miss your corrections when you transfer them to the computer. Red or blue stand out well, but as long as the colour is a good contrast to the text, go for it.

White Out – We all make mistakes when we're marking corrections. Obliterating them is often better than lots of confusing crossings-out.

Dictionary and Grammar Book – If you're not one hundred per cent sure about a spelling or a grammar point, you should always look it up.

A Decent Lamp – You will need a good source of light by which to work – reading in such detail can be very tiring on the eyes.

Style Sheet – Remember at the beginning of this book we talked about creating a style sheet? You may already have added some items to it. Always keep it by you when you are proofreading so that you can quickly check a particular point.

WHEN AND WHERE

Proofreading properly takes a lot of concentration. It cannot be carried out effectively in the lounge with the kids playing computer games and your partner watching TV. You need to find a quiet place where you can give the task your full attention.

If you don't have an office, try using the bedroom. Or try doing your proofreading early in the morning before anyone else is up (or late at night if you're a night owl). What about when the kids are at school? Can you grab an hour then?

You also need to have a decent amount of time to dedicate to the task. Five minute bursts of work are really no good to you. However, too long spent proofreading at one time will also be detrimental to the quality of your work. Limit yourself to one to two hours at a time, taking at least half an hour's break between sessions.

Turn off all distractions – and that means your eMail and your mobile phone. Any disturbance will take you out of your rhythm.

GETTING STARTED

Three hundred or so pages of a manuscript in a pile in front of you can be extremely daunting. No, scrub that – it is daunting. It is also impractical to work from a pile of paper several inches high. Place your manuscript in front of you a single page at a time. Have the main pile to one side and the completed pile to the other.

Start by placing your ruler under the first line of text (and that means the front matter – it all needs proofreading) and read the text slowly and deliberately. Read it line-by-line. Say it out loud as you go if that helps. When you move from one line to another, be careful to check that the sentence flows. When you have read the first paragraph, go back and re-read it in its entirety for sense. Then go onto the next paragraph, line-by-line.

Mark any corrections or queries clearly. Don't forget to use a colour other than black – your manuscript may look like it's bleeding if you use red, but at least you'll know where the wounds are.

Use correction symbols if you feel comfortable with them. Otherwise, make a clear mark in the text and write the correction in full in the margin (see How to Mark Corrections below for further information).

Make sure that you don't skim over the last line of a paragraph, or the last line of a page, because you are eager to get onto the next one. Consciously force yourself to read more slowly at these points in the text.

Read from the beginning of the manuscript to the end over a period of several days. If you interrupt the process by starting to update your electronic document before you have finished proofreading, you are likely to miss problems with consistency because your mind is no longer focussed.

ONE THING AT A TIME

Don't try and do everything at once, because you will never manage it until you are much more experienced at proofreading. Split your proofreading work into different tasks and stick to those tasks, completing them in separate passes of your manuscript (there is no need to do separate print-outs for this – all corrections can be placed on the same copy). I would suggest tackling the text in the following order:

Pass One – Check for spelling, grammar and punctuation errors;

Pass Two – Check the text for formatting, such as paragraph indents, spacing, alignment, etc;

Pass Three – Check for consistency in headings (including headlines in a print version);

Pass Four – Check page numbers against the contents page, index, etc (where appropriate, ie, a print version).

HOW TO MARK CORRECTIONS

When professional proofreaders mark text with corrections they make two types of mark. One is in the actual text and one in the margin. The mark in the text is an indication of where the correction needs to be made. The mark in the margin is the actual correction.

This technique makes it much easier to write the corrections out, by avoiding tiny writing squashed between lines of print, and much easier to read when you come to transfer the corrections to the electronic document.

I'm not suggesting for a moment that you should learn all of the standard correction symbols (unless you really want to), that is unnecessary as you will be the one transferring the corrections to the electronic document, but one or two could help you to avoid confusion.

The graphic below gives an example of some symbols that may be of use to you. These are not all strictly standard correction symbols as there are symbols to indicate capital letters, rather than just writing a letter in capitals.

As you can see, the symbols and the text in the margins go in the order of the corrections across the line of text, so that you can tell which mark corresponds to which correction. If you don't do this, you could confuse yourself when transcribing to your electronic copy.

(NB: *You will notice that I have used black corrections with black text for this graphic because this publication is not being printed in full colour. Notice how it is more difficult to see the corrections when they are the same colour as the text.*)

TRANSCRIPTION

Transcription is the term used for transferring your corrections from the print copy to the electronic document.

You need to be as careful when you transcribe your corrections as you were when you were marking them up. Make sure that you continue to use your ruler as you follow the text down the page. That way you will ensure that you don't miss anything.

Don't rush. If you do, you may miss corrections or introduce further errors that will then need to be corrected.

Read through each sentence after you have corrected it to make sure that you have transcribed everything.

If you find a page where you haven't marked any corrections at all, give it one extra check – especially if all your other pages have multiple corrections to make.

CHECK AND CHECK AGAIN

Once you have transcribed all your corrections, print out the text again. Then check that all the corrections have been made line-by-line.

To do this place the two pages of text side-by-side (corrected copy and clean copy) and use a ruler on each page to follow the lines down the page. If you find you have missed something, mark it on the clean copy and carry on until you get to the end of the document. Then transcribe and check again.

Continue until your manuscript is perfect.

WORDS AND NUMBERS

Now we are going to concentrate on the types of errors we are looking for and how to spot them. We'll start with what we read first – the words and numbers.

Please note that, although I will highlight some of the grammatical points and spelling errors you need to look out for, this is not a grammar book or a dictionary. These are merely pointers and prompts. You should always have a grammar book and a dictionary beside you when proofreading.

SPELLING ERRORS AND TYPOS

Whether you're a A-grade speller or not, we all have words that we are un-sure of how to spell correctly or combinations of letters that we always type in the wrong order – however hard we try to avoid it. (Why do you think that Microsoft Word has standard AutoCorrections set for adn and teh? Because we all do it.) Then, there are the words that are correct, but you look at what you've typed and it just looks wrong. Even when you look the word up in the dictionary, you're still not convinced. Good old, silly old brains again. If you read your manuscript line-by-line you are much more likely to pick up all of these errors.

If you are at all unsure about the spelling of a word, please always check it in the dictionary. It may be a word that can be spelled in different ways depending on context, or a word that has different meanings for the differ-ent spellings. Or there may even be two completely interchangeable spellings – in this case, pick one and use it consistently throughout your manuscript. Treat the dictionary as your friend, not your enemy.

For those of you who don't like the time it takes to leaf through a paper dictionary, you might want to download a proper electronic dictionary (I mean one that you pay for, not the freebies available on your browser). I have an electronic dictionary and I love it. It answers any queries I have in seconds and it even suggests the correct word if I get the spelling wrong (a paper dictionary can't do that). And it has this nifty little function that lets you look up the conjugation of any verb – great for those irregular verbs that the English language is so fond of. This type of dictionary won't be right for everyone – use what you are comfortable with, but do use it.

The types of spelling errors that are the most difficult to see are:

- Extra repeat letters in a word (ie, triple letters instead of doubles, such as illlicit – the 'i's either side make this one even more difficult to spot);
- Words that exist, but are the wrong words (small words can be especially difficult to spot, eg, if, it, is, in);
- Words that exist, but have a different meaning (eg, affect and effect);
- Errors in longer words (your eye might gloss over them quickly if they are familiar and appear many times in the text, eg, in this book that might be something like misspelling manuscript);
- Transposed letters (ie, the order of two letters has been swapped, eg, guage instead of gauge)

Some of the examples above would never be picked up in a simple computer spell check because they are real words, so extra care is needed.

Commonly Misspelled Words

Below is a small selection of words that are commonly misspelled. Are any of these ones that you have problems with?

Accommodate	Lightning
Committed	Maintenance
Definitely	Mischievous
Embarrassed	Occasionally
Environment	Privilege
Gauge	Questionnaire
Government	Rhythm
Independent	Separate
Liaison	

As you can see, many of them have double letters, silent letters or their pronunciation suggests a different letter.

Proofreading Checklist

✓ Make a list of the correct spellings of words you frequently have difficulty with and keep it with your style sheet. Then, you won't have to look them up in a dictionary every time you need to check them. Of course, the other option is never to use words that you're not sure of how to spell. But that would be silly, wouldn't it?

MISUSED WORDS

The term misused words covers a wide range of different circumstances. The link between them is that the user didn't understand the meaning of the word they were using (we're not talking here about your fingers getting in a muddle and typing 'it' instead of 'in'). However, they probably thought that they did understand the meaning, because they've been using it that way for years, and no amount of proofreading your own manuscript is going to overcome that. If you know you're bad with misusing words, get someone else to go through your manuscript, even if it's only a friend, your mother or a work colleague. And always, always, always look up words you're not sure about.

Below, is a breakdown of the different types of commonly misused words.

Similar Sound – Different Meaning

There are many words that sound or look similar to other words in the English language. In speech, you might not notice the difference, but when writing, you need to get it right. It is also very easy to type the wrong one by mistake when you're on a roll – so even if you do know the difference, double-check them in your manuscript anyway.

Below is a sample list of some of the most common similar sounding words that people get wrong.

Accept and except	Lead and led
Adverse and averse	Lie and lay
Affect and effect	Lightening and lightning
Allusion and illusion	Loose and lose
Assure, ensure and insure	No and know
Bear and bare	Of and off
Bought and brought	Passed and past
Cite, site and sight	Peak, peek and pique
Complement and compliment	Personal and personnel
Council and counsel	Plain and plane
Desert and dessert	Principle and principal
Discreet and discrete	Seem and seam
Elicit and illicit	Shear and sheer
Emigrate and immigrate	Stationery and stationary
Fair and fare	Tail and tale
Farther and further	Their, there and they're
Foreword and forward	To, too and two
Here and hear	Your and you're
It's and its	Weather and whether

Proofreading Checklist

- ✓ If there are any words in the list above that you don't know the meaning of, look them up now and find out how they are used.
- ✓ Search the internet for other lists of commonly misused words and note down the correct use of any that you don't know and might use in your writing. Read them through again and again so that when they appear in your manuscript they trigger that double-check button in your head.

Similar Letters – Wrong Word

This often occurs when letters are transposed or a letter is missed out as you type, but what you have typed still makes a word. Here are some examples:

Casual and Causal	Friend and Fiend	Table and Tablet
Diary and Dairy	Quite and Quiet	

Proofreading Checklist

- ✓ These are incredibly difficult to spot because your mind is going to do that 'filling in what it expects to see' thing again.
- ✓ If you find one instance in your manuscript, try a Find and Replace on the word to make sure you haven't repeated the mistake. Once you have got a word wrong once, you will often mistype it again.

Words You Always Mistype

We all have these. If you are a touch typist you will probably realise the error as you type the word, if not, you will need another solution.

Proofreading Checklist

- ✓ Make a list of the words you always mistype and keep it with your style sheet as a memory jogger.
- ✓ Try putting the words into the AutoCorrect Function in your word processor, unless your mistype is another actual word (as in Similar Letters – Wrong Word above), so that even if you do mistype them, they won't appear in your manuscript.

Wrong Context

Another common error is to use a word you think is correct in a particular situation, but it isn't. These are not necessarily words that look or sound the same. This kind of misuse can sometimes be caused by an over-reliance on the thesaurus to bring variety to your text. Does that sound like something you might do? It can also occur because some words are so frequently misused that we just assume the misuse is correct.

Some examples of commonly misused words are listed below. Once again, look them up if you don't know when they should be used:

Acute and chronic;   Literally;
Fewer and less;   Ultimate.
Ironic;

Proofreading Checklist

✓ If you use a thesaurus to find alternative words, make sure that you look up the word in a dictionary as well before you use it and if you can find some examples of correct use, so much the better.

✓ Make a list of any words you find you have used incorrectly and keep it as a reference sheet.

✓ Remember that simple is often better – when we try to be clever, we sometimes get it wrong.

Not When Writing

You have probably used these two words in this form for most of your life – language develops and modern usage of these words has changed how they are commonly spelled. However, when writing, it is generally considered better to use the older form indicated here in brackets:

Alright (All right);
OK (Okay).

Proofreading Checklist

✓ A simple use of the Find and Replace Function should sort this one out – but don't forget that 'ok' could well be part of another word.

Just Wrong

Finally, we have words and phrases that are often used, but either don't exist, or the person has misheard them and made an assumption about the spelling – an incorrect assumption. Below are a few examples. The correct form is in brackets. If you don't know why they are wrong, look them up:

Alot (A lot);
Irregardless (Regardless);
Hone in (Home in);
I could care less (I couldn't care less);
Could of (Could have);

Would of (Would have);

Baited breath (Bated breath);

For all intensive purposes (For all intents and purposes);

Bare in mind (Bear in mind).

Proofreading Checklist

✓ If you think that you have made some of these mistakes in your text, use the Find and Replace Function to search them out, and add them to your list of words and phrases to look out for in the future.

✓ Think carefully about any verbs after which you have placed the word 'of'. Should it be have? Might of and may of come to mind as other potential errors.

Getting Technical

Be careful when using technical words and industry-specific jargon if you are not completely sure of the proper meaning. If you use these words incorrectly, you can be certain that the world's greatest expert on that subject will be the first one to choose your book from that virtual shelf and pick you up on it.

If you're using the latest business jargon in your book, bear in mind that it may be a buzz phrase for only a short period of time, maybe even less than a year. Do you want to date your book in that way? Your choice. (This could also be an issue when referring to technology. How long will it be before the next big thing takes over from the kind of phone you use now?)

Proofreading Checklist

✓ If you have to use technical language, and you are not an expert, ask someone who is to check over the text where this language is used.

✓ Consider carefully whether or not to use jargon.

Text Speak

I would strongly advise against using text speak in your work, even if you do have characters constantly texting each other. Many people will not understand it and you will limit your readership. If you really feel you have to use it, intersperse the odd text word with normal spellings to give a feel for the language rather than using it for every word.

Proofreading Checklist

✓ Make sure you use consistent spelling for each term. Perhaps keep a list of the text words you are going to include.

✓ Only use terms that will be recognised by the majority of people. If readers have to think about what something means, you have taken them out of the story – and they may give up on it.

✓ Don't use terms that might have more than one potential meaning. (Remember how the UK's Prime Minister, David Cameron, reportedly misinterpreted LOL? He thought it was lots of love, in case you didn't know.)

MISSING WORDS

When you're typing at speed, it is very easy to miss out a word completely. It's another one of those things that happens when your brain is going faster than your fingers. Such errors can also be caused by changing text during the editing process.

Proofreading Checklist

✓ Don't forget to read every sentence through twice, the first time for errors and then again, as part of a whole paragraph, for sense.

✓ Words that are particularly easy to miss out are the very small words, such: as, the, it, if, is, in, etc.

?

It's spot the deliberate error time again. Did you see that one?

There should have been the word 'as' after such in the checklist point above this section. Actually, there was, but it was after the colon, so your brain might have compensated. If you caught it – well done.

EXTRA WORDS

Editing your text can also introduce extra words. One stray word can remain in the middle of a sentence that no longer makes sense.

It is also common to find doubled-up words lurking in the text, eg, the the. The doubled-up word can be particularly difficult to spot when it is split over two lines (and, of course, that is where it will always appear – Mr Murphy has a lot to answer for).

Proofreading Checklist

✓ As with missing words, these should jump out at you when you read the text for sense, or you might be able to catch them by the reading out loud or reading backwards methods.

✓ Take extra care when reading from one line, or one page to the next. It can be easy to miss doubled-up words when they are split up.

REPEATED WORDS

What I mean by repeated words are the usually longer, significant words (or phrases) that might appear two or three times within a paragraph. This is bad style and should be avoided either by using an alternative word, or by cutting them out completely. For example:

What I mean by repeated words are usually the longer, significant words (or phrases) that may be repeated two or three times within a paragraph. This type of repeated word is bad style and should be avoided either by using an alternative word, or by cutting the repeated word out completely.

Obviously, the paragraph above is an extremely bad case of repetition, but you'll probably be surprised how often you do repeat a noun or an adjective several times within a few lines of text without realising it. Keep an eye out for it, and change the offending words where you can.

This kind of error is much easier to change in a novel than a non-fiction 'How to' book. I'm trying hard not to type proofreading too many times in this manuscript, for example. Oops, there's another one – manuscript.

Proofreading Checklist

✓ The only way you can avoid this error is by reading your text through a paragraph at a time. You are more likely to spot it when reading out loud.
✓ Another person reading your manuscript is also more likely to find this kind of repetition.

TRANSPOSED WORDS

Transposed words are when the words in the sentence are in the wrong order, eg, He knew that was it wrong. They can be very difficult to find because they fall into the brain compensating category we have already discussed.

Proofreading Checklist

✓ The only way you can find these is by reading the text for sense – there is no easy fix. If you're lucky, your word processor might have under-lined the words for you, but mine didn't with my incorrect sentence.
✓ Reading out loud might help you catch these errors.

DIALOGUE TAGS

Your dialogue tags really should have been sorted out during the editing stage. However, it's always good to give things one final look over.

If you notice a whole conversation where dialogue tags are included on every piece of speech, think very carefully about whether they are all needed. If the conversation is between two people, you can probably ditch a few. If there are three or more people talking, they may well be necessary.

Proofreading Checklist

✔ Checking for excessive use of dialogue tags might be better done by a friend or a beta reader. If they can understand what is going on without the tags, then they are unnecessary.

NUMBERS

What you need to decide about numbers is whether or not you will always write them out in full when they appear in your text, or whether you will use a combination of words and figures.

If you choose the first option, it's easy – and I think this is the most sensible way to deal with figures in a novel, as they are unlikely to appear very often. If you decide to use a mixture – a more suitable option for non-fiction – you need to decide where your threshold for changing from written numbers to figures is (usually ten or one hundred). You also need to ensure that you don't introduce any strange combinations by following your rules too strictly. For example, if you were discussing a speed range of eighty to one hundred and one, and your threshold was one hundred, writing 80 to one hundred and one would be a little odd. Choose one format for both (80–101 is probably the most sensible).

There are many rules relating to numbers (please look them up for a complete overview). Here are some of the ones that you are most likely to need:

- Write out a number when it starts a sentence;
- Hyphenate written, two-part numbers between twenty-one and ninety-nine;
- Use figures with measurements and make sure that the measurement is singular, eg, 75 cm (use a non-breaking space between the unit and the measurement to keep them together);
- For ease of reading, punctuate numbers or use thin spaces, eg, 1,000,000 or 1 000 000 (but do make sure that any spaces are non-breaking spaces);

- Link number ranges in figures with an en dash, not a hyphen (see Hyphens and Dashes);
- Do not use an apostrophe in plurals, eg, 1960s;
- Use figures for currencies;
- Use figures for times with am and pm (use a non-breaking space to keep the figures and the am or pm together).

Proofreading Checklist

✓ Ensure that all your numbers follow the threshold rule you have set.
✓ Check that any abbreviated measurements are singular, eg, cm and not cms. If you know what measurements you have used you could use Find and Replace to check this.
✓ Check that you have correctly hyphenated written numbers from twenty-one to ninety-nine. You could use Find and Replace for this one with each ten (eg, twenty, thirty).
✓ Keep an eye out for odd combinations.

PUNCTUATION

Punctuation errors can be very easy to miss. To a certain extent, this is because punctuation marks are so small and they disappear into the mass of letters on the page. However, there are also many technical errors people make, and before we actually go into the details of checking punctuation, there's something I would like to highlight.

There are no spaces between the end of a sentence and a punctuation mark, before a comma, between a word and the related apostrophe, before and after a slash, or between a bracket and the text within it. The only punctuation mark that has spaces either side is an ellipsis. You wouldn't put a space between the last letter of a sentence and a full stop, so why do it with a question mark or an exclamation mark? If you do, you could see the punctuation appearing on a separate line in an eBook and, no doubt, you would wonder why. Get rid of all those extra spaces now.

Although you are unlikely to have missed a full stop completely, you might well have typed a comma instead, which would be very easy to mistake by proofreading on the screen. It isn't surprising that people make this error without realising it, the two keys are right next to each other on the keyboard and if you're not a touch typist you are much more likely to have hit the wrong key by mistake.

It is also very easy to use too many commas, but it is just as bad to have too few commas – people need to breathe while they're reading, even if it is only in their heads.

Common punctuation errors that are difficult to spot are:

- Commas instead of full stops (or vice-versa);
- Missing or unnecessary apostrophes;
- Inconsistencies with using full stops (or not) with abbreviations;
- The second bracket in a set;
- Missing question mark at the end of a sentence;

- Missing quotation marks or commas in a long piece of dialogue, especially when interspersed with narrative.

There is another thing you might want to look out for in punctuation. You might not have ever noticed this, but punctuation marks in traditionally published books are always in plain text. That means, if you have a phrase in, for example, italicised text, and you have quotation marks around it, the quotation marks are always in plain text. Likewise, an apostrophe in the middle of an italicised phrase will be in plain text. The only instance in which the character would be in the formatted text, is if it were integral to the text, eg, *that's life!* magazine in the UK has the apostrophe and exclamation mark as part of its name, so they should be italicised.

If you want your book to look as professional as possible, you should consider making these changes in your document. However, I can tell you from experience that they are very difficult to spot. What you really need is a print-out of how these punctuation marks look in both forms, like I have demonstrated below.

Comma	Apostrophe	Quotation mark	Semi-colon
, ,	' '	" "	; ;
Colon	Question mark	Exclamation mark	Slash
: :	? ?	! !	/ /

The difference on some is more subtle than others (and the quotation marks and apostrophes look almost the same when I do this on my eReader) and you might not feel that you want to go into this detail. That is entirely up to you and, realistically, most readers are unlikely to notice the difference. But if you want your manuscript to look really professional, it is the little things that matter.

Of course, there are also errors in terms of misused punctuation to look out for. Use your grammar book if you are uncertain on how to use punctuation correctly. Particular areas you need to be confident in are:

- Use of colons and semi-colons (excessive use of semi-colons is often frowned upon – try splitting the text into two sentences or use a dash);
- Avoiding the comma splice (this is where two distinct sentences are joined by a comma);

- Avoiding run-on sentences (this is where two sentences, or more, are joined without any dividing punctuation);
- Hyphenation (see Incorrect End-of-Line Hyphenation below);
- Dialogue (see Dialogue below);
- Use of apostrophes (see Misused Apostrophes below).

Although a lot of readers might not pick up on this type of error, a particularly vocal number will and a publisher or agent most certainly will.

Proofreading Checklist

✓ Whenever you see a semi colon in your text, stop and think about whether you really need it. A semi-colon tends to weaken the force of the words after the semi-colon – a full stop might be better. Try not to have more than one appearing every few pages.

✓ With specific regard to proofreading for the comma splice or run-on sentences, consider the following. If you have a lot of very long sentences in your manuscript, it is possible that you have joined sentences together incorrectly. Read them through carefully. Are they really two different sentences? If you can split them up, do. However, be warned – you may also have joined two very short sentences together.

✓ If you run out of breath when reading, you probably need to break up your sentences more.

✓ Check brackets and quotation marks carefully. Look for the closing marks without reading the words in between to help spot omissions.

MISUSED APOSTROPHES

Apostrophes deserve to be highlighted separately because a lot of errors are made with them. Just look at the handwritten signs (and sometimes the printed ones) on your High Street – it's like they have rampant apostrophe disease.

Getting your apostrophe use wrong is highly likely to attract a tirade of abuse about your punctuation. I'm not sure why that is, it's such an innocent looking punctuation mark, but it might just be that it stands out more than anything else. For a start, it's above the line and the only other characters in that visual space are quotation marks.

The situations in which apostrophes are frequently misused are:

- Plurals;
- Possession;
- Decades;

- Acronyms;
- Abbreviations.

The complete rules on apostrophes are far to lengthy to go into here. If you don't know them, look them up, but here are a few pointers on the most common errors:

- Apostrophes are not required with plurals of years, eg, 1960s;
- Apostrophes are not required with plurals of abbreviations, eg, DVDs, PCs;
- Apostrophes are not required when creating a simple plural of a noun, eg, dogs, not dog's;
- The apostrophe should be before the 's' with a singular noun when indicating possession, eg, The dog's bone.
- When indicating possession with a plural noun, if the plural ends in an 's', the apostrophe goes after the word, if it ends with another letter, the apostrophe goes before the 's', eg, The people's choice; The writers' forum;
- It's only ever means it is or it has. It never indicates possession.

Proofreading Checklist

✔ Don't rely on what you see around you in daily life to guide you on apostrophe use – many people get it wrong.

✔ If you know that you often misuse an apostrophe in, for example, it's, do a Find on the word and replace it where necessary. Whatever you do, don't do a global replace, because then you'll change all the correct usage as well.

✔ Question every apostrophe you have used. Substitute the long version of the words, if it's a contraction. That should highlight if you have used you're instead of your, for example.

?

Okay, you know the deal with this by now. There is an incorrect 'to' in the text above. Did you see it?

If not, why not go back to the beginning of the section and find it?

DIALOGUE

Dialogue is another area where a lot of errors are made. Please ensure you know the rules for punctuating it correctly. A summary of the main ones you will need is below – for more detailed information, please refer to your grammar book:

- You should usually have a punctuation mark before your closing quotation mark;
- If you continue your sentence with a dialogue tag, that punctuation mark should be a comma, unless it is a question or an exclamation – it should not be a full stop;
- There should always be punctuation after the dialogue tag (or narrative), before the next speech (eg, "Dialogue," she said, "I hate it.");
- If a piece of dialogue ends the sentence (ie, there is no tag or narrative after it), the full stop will usually be within the quotation marks.

You will have to decide on which type of quotation marks you are going to use – double or single. Both are correct, but you need to be consistent. Whichever one you choose, the opposite will be used for thoughts, if you decide to put these in quotation marks. (*NB: UK printing conventions are normally single quotes and US are normally double quotes.*)

Some experienced writers don't use quotation marks at all. However, if you don't use them, your readers might get confused as to who is talking, or even if they are talking. As a new writer, I would suggest you stick with standard format.

Proofreading Checklist

✓ Make sure that each speaker starts on a new line.

✓ Check that each piece of dialogue has a punctuation mark.

✓ If you have a split section of dialogue, eg, with a dialogue tag, ensure the correct punctuation is inserted before the next piece of speech.

✓ In a long piece of speech, ensure that you have both opening and closing quotation marks.

ABBREVIATIONS AND FULL STOPS

When you use abbreviations, you have a decision to make with regards to consistency. You either use a full stop after them, or you don't. You shouldn't chop and change depending on the circumstances.

These days it is far more common to see abbreviations without a full stop. In fact, for many years it has been old-fashioned to put a full stop after Mr and Mrs or etc in the UK.

I know some of you will be querying this. You often see a letter addressed to you with a full stop after the Ltd (or Inc) in the company name and yet no full stop after the Mr (or many different variations on this). Stylistically, this is wrong and it shouldn't be done. Don't fall into the trap of, 'Well, everyone else does it, so I'll just follow them.' Make a choice and stick to it.

If you have an instance of the abbreviation not being clear without punctuation, write it out in full, eg, Fig could mean figure or an exotic fruit. If you're writing about fig production in the US, you could be in trouble.

Proofreading Checklist

✓ Keep a list of all the abbreviations you have used in your text as you write and do a Find and Replace on them when you are proofreading. You will easily be able to correct any misused, or missing, full stops this way.

HYPHENS AND DASHES

In traditional publishing several different types of dashes are used. The hyphen is a short line joining two words (or splitting them at the end of a line). There is also the en dash, which is a little bigger than a hyphen and the em dash, which is much longer. The en and the em dash are largely interchangeable, depending on a publisher's house style.

Hyphen	En dash	Em dash
-	–	—

Microsoft Word will implement a normal hyphen when you put it immediately between two words, eg, self-publishing. It will implement an en dash when you separate it with spaces either side from words – like this. If you type two hyphens together with no spaces—you get an em dash. All these formats are acceptable in the instances shown in publishing.

Hyphens are becoming less common in books. If the meaning is clear, they can sometimes be omitted. However, there are many instances where hyphens should be used for clarity. You'll need to look them up in your grammar book for a full explanation as the instances are far too complex to go into here.

En dashes are usually used when text is joined with spaces either side (as above) and to join two figures together.

Em dashes are usually used when there are no spaces either side of a dash (as above) and at the end of interrupted speech, although spaces can be added either side if required.

Proofreading Checklist

✓ Many dictionaries will be able to help you with whether or not a phrase should be hyphenated and it may be quicker than checking in your grammar book.

✓ Long strings of hyphenated words can be a problem in an eBook, so try not to use them unnecessarily simply for emphasis. Err on the side of less is better in this instance.

✓ Be consistent with which type of dash you use in each circumstance.

THE ELLIPSIS

If you are using an ellipsis in your text, remember that it should be only three dots (...). If the ellipsis comes at the end of a sentence you can include the sentence punctuation, so four dots is acceptable, but there should be a space between the three and the one as there is always one space either side of an ellipsis (eg, ...). In this instance, you will need to make the space a non-breaking space so that you don't end up with one full stop on its own on a line. It would also be a good idea to make it non-breaking to the word before it.

There is a Special Character in Microsoft Word (Alt+Ctrl+.) which places an ellipsis without having to press the full stop three times (eg, ...). If you use this you will need to make sure it translates properly if you are converting your document to eReader format.

Proofreading Checklist

✓ Ensure correct punctuation is inserted if an ellipsis is at the end of a sentence.

✓ It can be difficult to determine whether there are spaces either side of an ellipsis. If you aren't sure, mark it and use the Show/Hide Function in Microsoft Word to clarify when you come to transcribe your corrections.

QUESTIONS

Are all your questions actually questions? What I mean is, have you missed any question marks?

This is very easy to do when you are typing and can be difficult to spot even when you are reading out loud.

Proofreading Ch5ecklist

✓ If you often find you have missed question marks where they should have been placed, try putting in a Find search for all the words that can start a question (one at a time obviously) with a capital letter and look at all the sentences where they appear (eg, Why, When, Who). It won't necessarily catch all instances, but could help.

EXCLAMATIONS

Overuse of exclamation marks is frowned upon in writing. Some people say that you should never use them because the exclamation should be implied by the words used and the situation – that may be a little harsh. However, if you have them appearing on every page, you do have a problem.

Also, don't ever have more than one in a row (eg, !!!). That might be all right in a status update on a social network, but is completely incorrect in written English.

Proofreading Checklist

✓ Once again, you could use a Find search to locate them and then make the decision about whether or not they are necessary.

OTHER TEXT CONSISTENCY ISSUES

We've already talked about some consistency issues above, but there are several other things you need to check in your text. Some of these inconsistencies are things that readers probably won't consciously notice, but will niggle at their brain telling them that not everything was right with your book.

BRITISH VS AMERICAN SPELLING

Firstly, I do realise that there are more English-speaking nationalities than British and American, but it would be cumbersome to repeat the whole list each time, so please substitute your English-speaking country as appropriate.

Although a British reader will probably not be put off by American spellings (or vice versa), if the spelling nationalities are mixed up, it will confuse them (maybe even annoy them) and that is never a good thing. Don't do it.

One of the worst things you can do is attempt to adapt your text to American English if you're British, or British English if you're American, in the false hope that you can write specifically for a particular market. You might, if you're lucky, manage to get all the words spelled correctly, but you are unlikely to be able to phrase your sentences in a way that will truly pass your text off as written by someone of that nationality. If you absolutely have to do this, you need to get an editor and a proofreader from that country to convert your text for you.

However, there are some words where both spelling variants are used in the UK and the USA, for example, learnt and learned, spelt and spelled (the first being the so-called preferred British spelling and the second being the American). These words are often used interchangeably by people in each country, depending on how they are feeling at the time. In these instances, choose one and stick to it. Neither is wrong, but consistency is the most important thing.

Proofreading Checklist

- ✓ Make sure that your word processor is set to the correct language so that it will highlight any potential misspellings according to that particular version of English.
- ✓ If you know of any words you always spell the wrong way, use a Find and Replace to get rid of them.

-ISE VS -IZE SPELLING

This is often quoted as one of the differences between British and American spelling, with -ise being the British spelling and -ize being the American spelling, but that is not strictly true. Many dictionaries will tell you that they are both acceptable in each country, although as a Brit, I do always use -ise. There are, in fact, many books produced by British publishing houses that conform to -ize spelling, because it is their house style.

So, decide on your house style and stick to it.

If you don't know what I mean by this type of spelling, consider the following words. How would you spell them?

Civilisation or Civilization   Capitalised or Capitalized
Specialise or Specialize   Symbolise or Symbolize.

You probably naturally do one or the other.

Proofreading Checklist

- ✓ The only way to check for these is by reading through your text very carefully – and now that you know there is a difference, seeing the wrong version should trigger something in your brain.
- ✓ You might want to try and create a list of words that fall into this category, or where you're not sure if they fall into it or not.

PROPER NOUNS

There is more than one type of error that can occur when using proper nouns.

If we're talking about character names, then you might have spelled the name differently in different parts of the text by mistake (eg, Alec to Alex), or, even worse, you might have changed the character's name completely halfway through without realising it. It is much easier than you might think to make this kind of error.

Another common error with proper nouns is consistent capitalisation. In particular, this occurs when using the names of institutions, organisations, etc. With made-up names you simply need to ensure that they are consistently capitalised. However, if they really exist, making sure you capitalise as the institution does on their own logo or letterhead is important. Whether it is sensible to use real company names in your fiction is another issue entirely, although it is often necessary in non-fiction.

Proofreading Checklist

- ✔ Use Find and Replace to find names and check their spelling. Try putting in variations and see if they come up.
- ✔ Check all real company names on their official website.
- ✔ Every time a name appears, try to consciously think, 'Is this the right name?'

FORMATTING ELEMENTS

As mentioned earlier, checking the formatting of a book is an important part of the proofreading process, but, in this new world of self-publishing, there are different technical requirements depending on which format you are publishing in. Where appropriate, I have divided information into eBook or POD formatting requirements, but please make sure you read the instructions on the retailer's website as well, as they are all slightly different.

TEXT

It is important to get the layout of the body text of your document displayed well, as this is the bulk of what people will be reading.

The text itself needs to be in a standard font. That means not using any fancy fonts like script fonts or heavily emboldened fonts. These will often not be supported by the platform. The best fonts to use are your normal, everyday ones, like Times New Roman for eBooks, and Times New Roman, Arial, Garamond and Georgia for print books.

You also need to choose a standard font size – either 10, 11 or 12 pt, unless you are writing a book for young children in a fixed format.

If you choose something different from these suggestions, your book could end up looking unprofessional and possibly be unreadable.

eBook

Choosing a normal font and font size is particularly important for an eBook. Readers can change the size of the text if they need it larger to be able to read and on some eReaders they can also change the font. If you make the text a non-standard size, then it will display differently to other books and if the reader is flicking between reading a number of books at the same time (which is incredibly easy to do on an eReader) they will find it annoying if yours displays at a different size and they have to keep changing the font display size on their device.

You will also need to ensure that your font colour is not defined. What I mean by this is that your font colour needs to be on the Automatic setting. This displays as black when on a white background, but will also allow users to see white text on a black background, if they prefer that setting. If you define the text as black, when they change their settings to a black background, they will see nothing.

It is also advisable not to use other colours of text. On a black and white display these will show in shades of grey and might not be readable, depending on the amount of contrast.

Avoid using Special Characters and Symbols, if possible. These sometimes don't convert well in eBooks.

Proofreading Checklist

- ✓ Look at how your book displays compared to other books on your eReader. Do you have to change font size to read it?
- ✓ Try changing your eReader setting to white text on black. If any of the text disappears, you know you haven't got it set to Automatic.
- ✓ Check any Special Characters or Symbols, if you have used them, to ensure that they display correctly in all eBook formats.

POD

Your POD format document from the retailer will usually be set up with one of the standard fonts used in print publishing. Unless you have any great objection to that font, I would suggest keeping it as is – it has already been designed to look good.

Unless you are producing a colour book, keep all your fonts in black. I would use the actual Black setting in this context, rather than Automatic as any deviation from black in your document will register your book as full colour – and you don't want that as it will greatly increase the cost of producing it and reduce your royalty payments.

You can go as low as 10 pt text for a print book, but some people might find this difficult to read, depending on which font you have chosen. If you want to go smaller than 12 pt, I would opt for 11 pt as a compromise. (The text in this book is in 11 pt Garamond.)

Proofreading Checklist

- ✓ When you receive your proof copy, check that the text is easy to read. Don't rely on your own eyes. Ask around and see if your friends would be happy reading a whole book in the font and font size you have chosen.

INDENTS, SPACING AND ALIGNMENT

Although publishing uses several different forms of paragraph formatting, the traditional style for a novel is as follows:

- The first paragraph in any chapter, or section, is left-aligned (ie starts at the left-hand margin with no indent).
- Subsequent paragraphs are indented, traditionally by one em space.

I wouldn't expect anyone who is self-publishing to worry too much about how big an em space is (although if you think back to the em dashes, you can get a good idea), and it isn't something that is set in stone, as sometimes the indents used are bigger if house style dictates it, but the first paragraph at the left-hand margin is pretty standard. And keep in mind, if you use indented paragraphs, there is no line spacing between them.

Another formatting option is to have no indents at all. This is called block style. What you have to remember with this format is that you need to put a line space between each paragraph, otherwise the text becomes unreadable (it ends up looking like a single, giant paragraph). It is becoming more common to use block text in novels and can be essential for very short pieces, such as poetry or flash fiction, which don't have the balance on the page of much longer texts. It is much more often found in non-fiction books.

In the majority of books text is justified, that is, straight down left and right (apart from paragraph indents).

Many traditionally published books will also use drop caps at the beginning of a chapter. (See Drop Caps below.)

eBook

When formatting for an eBook, you must define your paragraphs using the Styles Function or the formatting might not translate properly when the document is converted.

For indented paragraphs you need to select a First Line Indent and define how big that indent is. Half a centimetre is fairly common.

For block paragraphs you also need to select a First Line Indent and set the indent amount to 0.01. This is because not all eReaders recognise the None indent setting (they revert to a standard indent when conversion takes place) and setting it at 0.01 fools the system and makes the indent so small that it is invisible to the naked eye.

For block paragraphs you also need to set Paragraph Spacing after the line (ie, when you press return the extra spacing will appear). If you don't set the spacing this way and simply press an extra return, your spacing may disappear during the conversion process. For this book I have used a 9 pt After setting for the eBook format.

Although your final converted eBook needs to be displayed as justified text, you need to make sure that all your paragraph text is left-aligned in your document. The conversion process will set your paragraphs to justified text and forcing it in your formatting could cause errors to appear.

If you need to define breaks in your text, ie, sections within your chapters, it is better not to do this by pressing returns (because once again, they may get lost in the conversion process and even if they don't, they may not be obvious to the reader if they fall at a page break on their screen).

Instead, try adding separators, such as:

***

or

###

to indicate breaks. Make sure you only use standard keyboard characters for this. Some of the Symbols available in Microsoft Word will not convert correctly. To my eye, centred always looks better for separators and that is the format you will find in traditionally published books. Leaving them left-aligned looks like the formatting has gone wrong.

POD

When preparing your document for POD you should also use the Styles Function and define your Paragraph Settings as specified above, although you can use the None setting for block paragraphs as this will not be affected during conversion (which is simply saving your document as a .pdf file). I have used a 6 pt after setting for my block paragraphs in the print version of this book.

Your paragraphs should be altered to make them justified, but make sure you don't select your headings when you do this or they might end up with some really weird spacing. The best way to change your text is to change your Normal Style to justified.

If you prefer, you can use returns to make breaks between sections rather than separators, as these will not be affected by conversion.

Proofreading Checklist

✔ It is often easier to do a separate pass on your document for formatting issues.

✔ Don't forget to check the first paragraph of every chapter or section to ensure it is left-aligned if you have used this format.

✔ Make sure all the indents are at the same level as each other (this should not be an issue if you have used the Styles Function).

✔ Make sure there is adequate spacing between paragraphs if you have chosen to use block style.

✔ After conversion to eBook, check that your paragraph formatting has worked in all formats available. For example, in Kindle format, display can be different from the phone app to the Kindle device. Bad formatting with your paragraphs will be very noticeable to a reader. Also, flick through your document to make sure that all the text is right justified.

✔ After receiving your POD proof, look through all the pages to ensure the formatting is correct. Don't skimp on this – if something has gone wrong in the production process you won't know if you don't check.

?

We were talking about consistent punctuation a few pages back. You might not have consciously noticed it, but I have been punctuating my clarifications and examples with a comma after the ie or eg. At the beginning of this section, there is an example of missing and inconsistent punctuation.

Did you see it? Can you see it now? It's in the first bullet point on the text within the brackets.

BULLETS AND NUMBERING

Most people will be familiar with the bulleted and numbered lists that you can create in Microsoft Word. These can be very useful in non-fiction texts to display information in an easy to digest format and are common in many traditionally published books.

You will need to decide on what kind of punctuation you want to use in your lists. It is common to have a colon before they start (at the end of the introducing sentence), but punctuation of the actual bullets varies. You could have semi-colons at the end of each line with a full stop on the last one, or you might prefer full stops on all of them or no punctuation at all.

You will also need to decide whether or not you want to start your bullet points with a capital letter or a lower case letter. Both are acceptable.

Above all, be consistent.

eBook

Unfortunately, at this time, Bullets and Numbering do not convert well into eBook formatting (although, I understand that it can be done more successfully if you are an expert in HTML code). Therefore, you will need to find a workaround.

If you do try to use indents, you will find that the text does not line up properly. All your indents will sit at slightly different levels because the text gets pulled across the page as a result of the justification (this is true for normal indents and hanging indents). This is ugly and I would suggest that you don't do it.

If you need to use bulleted or numbered lists, do the best you can, but accept that you might not get the text to look as perfect as you would like.

In the eBook version of this book, I have used a bullet marker (the em dash), without a space so that it is fixed to the text (and won't get pulled away from it by the justification), and have let the text wrap back to the margin.

POD

In a print book you can easily use the automatic Bullet and Numbering Functions. This means that, if you are converting from eBook, you are going to have to go through your whole manuscript and change whatever solution you used for your eBook into the correct format.

Be careful that you do not leave any of your old bullet markers behind – this is easily done – before pressing the Bullet Symbol.

Space your bullets out nicely. You could even indent the text on both left and right if book length is not an issue.

Proofreading Checklist

✓ In your print copy, ensure that your bullets are all indented to the same level and that no extra spacing has appeared. It is very easy to press the spacebar before starting to type your bullet point, for example.
✓ Check that the spacing between bullets is equal.
✓ Check that your bullet punctuation is consistent.

✓ If you are using bullets for your eBook, make sure your solution has worked reasonably well once you have converted your file. If not, you'll have to rethink your formatting. Check that the bullet marker you have chosen works in all eBook display formats (some Special Characters do not convert properly).

DROP CAPS

When I was talking about paragraph styles earlier, I mentioned drop caps. This is where a larger initial letter is inserted as the first letter of a chapter. It takes up the depth of two or three lines, which is why it is called a drop cap.

This format is more common in novels than non-fiction books. Have a look at novels in your genre to see whether it is common practice before deciding whether or not you want to teach yourself how to do it. But if you do decide to use drop caps, make doubly sure you use it for all your chapters.

Another thing to consider is that you don't necessarily need to stick to the same font as your main text for a drop cap. Sometimes this single letter use in a script-like font can be effective, if it suits the tone of your book.

Below is a very simple example of a drop cap set to drop across two lines of text and formatted in a different font to the body text.

*T*he first paragraph of a chapter may also have a Drop Cap (a larger initial letter that takes up the depth of two or three lines. In an eBook this might be substituted by using emboldened text for the first few words, usually in caps/small caps.

eBook

Drop caps are not usually inserted into eBooks because they don't always display well and you need to be experienced in coding HTML in order to do it properly. An alternative, for those who wish to make the initial text stand out, is to embolden a few words and/or make them all capital letters.

POD

Drop Caps are a good way to make your print book look like a traditionally published book. If you decide to use them, play around with a few styles first. Look at what each capital letter looks like in the font style you choose, sometimes script letters can be difficult to read. A 'T' might look really good and yet an 'I' might not.

Proofreading Checklist

✓ When checking for different chapter styling in an eBook, you can use your clickable Table of Contents to jump to the beginning of each chapter. Make sure that any emboldened or capitalised text is consistent throughout.
✓ In your print book flick through to each chapter beginning. Is there a drop cap on every one?

?

I'd be very surprised if you didn't see it, but did you notice the rogue indented text a few paragraphs back? Just checking.

SENTENCE SPACING

If you were taught to type back in the Dark Ages, like me, when there were no such things as personal computers and electric typewriters were beyond the means of most schools, then you were probably taught to put two spaces between sentences. I have bad news for you – this is a big no-no in publishing and you have to get out of the habit of doing it. I know it's difficult – I had to retrain myself to only press the spacebar once – but it's not impossible, and there will be a time when it becomes second nature. If I can train myself to change after typing with two spaces for thirty-five years, then so can you.

There is no situation where double spaces would be allowed in a traditionally published book and you would probably be asked to alter it before the editor even got their hands on your manuscript if you went via the traditional publishing route. So, if you want your book to look professional, you have to get rid of those extra spaces.

While you're retraining, use the Find and Replace Function, after you have completed your manuscript, to remove the extra spaces (yes, Find and Replace will search for spaces, there doesn't have to be text in the boxes – just press the spacebar twice in Find and once in Replace), and do this as the last task before printing out, because if you start typing again, you'll only introduce more spaces and they'll be even more noticeable because the rest have been changed to single spaces.

Proofreading Checklist

✓ Before you print out your document, do a Find and Replace for double-spacing. It may not only appear between sentences, but also between words. If you don't remove them, the justification of the text will look very gappy.

✓ Extra spaces can be difficult to spot in a print copy. If you find a space that looks too big, but you're not sure, mark it up. When you look at the electronic document, if you use the Show/Hide Function, every space will be shown as a dot (placed at about midway down the line, so you cannot confuse it with a full stop). If you see two or more of these next to each other, that indicates the number of spaces in the text. Make sure it is only one.

END-OF-LINE HYPHENATION

End-of-line hyphenation is used to even out the way words are spaced on the line to avoid excessive squashing or gapping when text is justified. The idea is to split the word in the most appropriate place so that it is still readable even though it is on two lines.

Below are some basic rules of hyphenation to help you:

- Look at the syllables in a word. The space between syllables is a natural break and is usually, but not always, a good place for a hyphen;
- Don't let the break of a word create different words that could be confusing – or embarrassing, eg, the-rapist is clearly inadvisable, but dish-cloth is not;
- A double letter can be a natural break, except when it comes in the middle of a syllable, eg, dis-sent would be okay, but cho-ose wouldn't;
- It is better to have at least three letters in each half of the word;
- Don't hyphenate the last word in a paragraph;
- Don't hyphenate a contraction that uses an apostrophe;
- Don't hyphenate proper nouns;
- A word within a hyphenated phrase should not be hyphenated, eg, south-west-ern;
- Books for young children should not be hyphenated;
- Don't use hyphenation at the end of three consecutive lines as this is confusing to the reader.

eBook

If you are publishing to eBook format, you should not implement end-of-line hyphenation. It is only relevant for a print book. However, you do need to ensure that it is turned off in your source document. If you leave the hyphenation function on, then hyphens may appear in your text in the eBook, but are unlikely to appear at the end of the line because of the reflowable nature of the text. It does happen. I've seen traditionally published books produced in eBook format where they have clearly used the print book master document and have not reformatted it, resulting in some very weird hyphenated words in the middle of a line.

POD

End-of-line hyphenation can be a useful tool when preparing a print book. Justification spreads out lines of text to fit the width of the page and if, for example, you have six long words next to each other, there may not be room to put more than five of them on a single line. The result without hyphenation will be that the gaps between the words will be made much larger in order to compensate.

You will notice that I said helped and not eliminated. This is because a word processing package is not a typesetting package. It will never be as good as a traditionally published book, but it will look better than it would look without hyphenation and, unless you compare typeset text side-by-side with word-processed text, most people won't notice the difference.

There are two options for using the Hyphenation Function in Microsoft Word. The first is Automatic. This will go through the whole of your document, without your input, and hyphenate the document where it is thought appropriate. It will follow whatever rules you set in the dialogue box. However, this will involve another whole round of intensive proofreading to ensure that the hyphens have not been placed in inappropriate places.

Another way of implementing Hyphenation is to put them in on the Manual setting. You will be prompted every time Microsoft Word finds a word it thinks should be hyphenated and you will be given the chance to accept or decline. You can then take a decision based upon the word, the look of the page and any other hyphenation on the page.

I would opt for Manual, but always do this right at the end, after all other proofreading, because if you change the wording, the Hyphenation will reset in the paragraph you have changed.

For the print version of this book, I implemented Hyphenation chapter-by-chapter. So, I made sure all the text was correct first, then I manually hyphenated the chapter and finally I sorted out things like widows and orphans and uneven page lengths.

Proofreading Checklist

✓ When using Hyphenation, check that the words have been split appropriately.

✓ If you find more than two consecutive lines with hyphens at the end, change the text to eliminate this as it will be confusing to your readers. (This could also happen if you have a hyphenated phrase and a word that has been split underneath each other.)

✓ If you have used Hyphenation, if you implement a change to a word you don't want hyphenated, all your hyphens in that paragraph may change. Manually hyphenate that paragraph again if you need to.

✓ Any hyphenation that takes your mind away from the text to look at the individual words is bad and needs to be eliminated.

WIDOWS AND ORPHANS

Widows and orphans are where the first line of a paragraph appears at the bottom of one page (orphan) or the last line of a paragraph appears at the top of a page (widow). It is not good style and, ideally, the text around it needs to be adjusted so that this doesn't happen.

eBook

Widows and orphans are not an issue that you can do anything about in an eBook, because the text is reflowable. They will appear all over the place and you will simply have to accept it.

POD

Widows and orphans in print books really should be sorted out. There are a number of ways that this can be done:

• Alter a phrase to remove or add a word or two. This will help to push over or pull back some text onto a different line.

• If you are using block style, you could alter your paragraph spacing between the paragraphs on your page. Changing it by 1 pt might be enough to resolve the problem and shouldn't be noticeable when compared to the opposite page.

• Use the Kerning Function to squeeze up some of the words (only useful if you have a single word on one line which you need to pull back).

(NB: *You might also be able to use these techniques if you find a heading sitting on its own at the bottom of a page which isn't very good style for a print book, or you might have to force it onto another page with a Page Break.*)

Remember when you do this that it will have a knock-on effect on subsequent pages in the same chapter. You may end up having to alter them as well.

Proofreading Checklist

- ✓ Widows and orphans are easy enough to spot in your POD document, but don't look for them until you have done your final proofread corrections for your print book.
- ✓ Deal with them one at a time and in document order as there may be knock-on effects later in the text.

PAGE SIZE

The page size of your book can be the size it is displayed at on an eReader or the print size you choose for a POD book. These vary considerably and you need to take this into account when designing how your book will look. It won't be the same for both formats, so be prepared to make some changes.

eBook

Page sizes for eBooks can be anything from a mobile phone screen to a PC screen, as downloadable apps are available for all of these. Therefore, it is extremely difficult to format your book so that it will look perfect on all of them.

I would suggest that you design your book for a normal eReader size. This will usually work well in larger formats. However, you will have to accept that it is unlikely to look perfect on a mobile phone. The mobile phone screen may not allow you to read more than three or four words to a line and only a few lines on a page. There are very few books that will work well on this size page. Some of this book won't display all that well, that's for sure.

Proofreading Checklist

- ✓ Ensure that you check the way your book displays on all platforms available – it won't display the same way on each.

POD

When you use POD, one of the first things you have to decide upon is the page size for your book. Until you have done this and downloaded the page format file, you cannot finalise anything else. Choose one and stick to it, or you'll create yourself a lot of extra and unnecessary work.

The page size will determine how many pages there are in your book. If you have long chapters, a slightly larger size might be appropriate. If you have lots of short chapters, you might find that a large size will mean a lot of empty half pages (or whole pages) which all adds to the cost of the book (not good when you're trying to attract customers by pricing attractively), so choose a smaller size.

Try measuring some of the books on your shelves and see what the usual size for books in your genre, or subject, is and go from there – there is no right or wrong answer, but you must make your final choice before beginning to format your text.

CHAPTERS

There are no hard-and-fast rules on how long a chapter should be. In a non-fiction book they are easy to define as the end of one topic, but in a novel it is down to the author to decide where the story should break. However, when it comes to formatting, a chapter should always start on a new page and it needs a title, even if that title is only the number one, for example.

eBook

In an eBook, new chapters are generally defined by a forced Page Break. Never simply use the return key to separate the text from the previous chapter as these returns will often be lost in the conversion process and won't necessarily push your chapter onto a new page anyway.

Before you insert your Page Break, ensure that you have pressed return at the end of your previous chapter text, otherwise the formatting will not be preserved correctly.

Chapters in an eBook start at the top of the page, no spacing is required and it should not be used.

POD

Chapters in a print book are a little more complicated.

Firstly, don't use a Page Break to define them, use a Section Break with the New Page setting. This will allow you to have different formatting in your document when you come to add Running Headlines and Page Numbers (see below). If you use a format document provided by the POD publisher the Sections should already be formatted for you.

You will need to ensure that every chapter starts on a right-hand page of your book (ie, an odd numbered page). However, in some books where the text in each chapter (or piece) is very short, such as poetry or flash fiction books, it is acceptable to have pieces start on even pages, or even to let them continue on the same page, otherwise a lot of paper would be wasted in printing. If this is not an issue for you, and display is important, then follow the odd pages rule for new pieces.

Also, it is common to drop the text further down the page at the start of a chapter – as much as halfway down in some books. This is much more attractive than starting right at the top of the page.

If you decide to do this, the easiest way to make sure they are all the same is to put Paragraph Spacing before your chapter title style, ie, Heading 1.

Proofreading Checklist

✓ Ensure that all chapters start on a new page.
✓ In your print copy, check each chapter starts on a right-hand page (where appropriate) and that all begin at the same level down the page.

HEADINGS

Headings need to stand out, whichever format you are producing your book in, and the different levels of heading need to be easily recognisable. This differentiation can be achieved by changing:

- Font and font size;
- Capitalisation method;
- Alignment;
- Emboldening or italics.

I have omitted underlining because I would strongly suggest that you don't use it. Apart from the fact that it is also used to indicate hyperlinks in eBooks and could cause confusion, some people with reading difficulties and impairments find it hard to read text that is underlined.

There are a number of different styles you can use for capitalisation:

- Initial cap on the first word only (although you will still need to capitalise any proper nouns that don't happen to be the first word);
- All caps (this keeps life simple and you can't really get it wrong);
- Capitals only on important words (explained below).

If you want to capitalise only the important words, there are a number of rules to follow (please note, there are variations on these rules according to the house style of a particular publisher). For our purposes, I'm going to define the rules as follows:

- Use capital letters for the first word and the last word of the title;

- Use capital letters for nouns and pronouns, adjectives, verbs and adverbs, and subordinating conjunctions;
- Don't use capital letters on small words, such as: a, and, at, by, for, in, it, of, on, the.

eBook

When formatting an eBook, headings should always be implemented by using the Styles Function (using Heading 1, 2, etc, for the different levels). You must use these pre-set styles for your headings or you will find that they don't convert to eBook format as you might have expected.

If you don't like the font style or font size of the pre-set styles you can modify them, but don't make them too big (maximum of 14 point, unless your headings are very short, eg, Chapter 1, Chapter 2, etc). Remember that you need to format so that your book is readable on all devices and a huge font for your title is going to look ridiculous on a mobile phone display.

Decide on whether you want your headings left-aligned or centred. Centring would be more standard for chapter headings in a novel, but a non-fiction book could be either (centring does have an advantage in eBooks as the text doesn't get stretched across the page when there are multiple line headings). I wouldn't suggest right-aligned for an eBook, it is likely to look odd on smaller displays and the reader might think it has been badly formatted.

You also need to consider how long your heading is. If it spans across three lines on a normal eBook display, it might be too long. If it spans more than one line, you might find that the software tries to justify the text on the first line and it will end up stretched across the screen.

Don't put returns into long headings. They need to be reflowable like your text and, unfortunately, that often means that multiple line headings will display unevenly. There is nothing you can do about this.

When I was formatting this book for the eBook version, I found that, on my basic Kindle eReader, emboldened text in Times New Roman (the font in this paragraph) did not stand out well in the titles once the document had been converted. Therefore, I changed to a completely different font – Arial. The Arial font is also a sans-serif font (doesn't have little tails on the letters), so that makes it stand out even more. Because I have several levels of heading, I used 14 pt for the chapters and 12 point for most other headings. Differentiation in an eBook can be difficult when multiple level headings are required and I wouldn't recommend doing this unless you have to, as you will find out later in this book when I recount some of my experiences after converting it to eBook format.

POD

When formatting for POD you can be a little more adventurous and visually pleasing with your headings. If you are converting your eBook file to print format, why not change your Heading Styles to something different? In a print version you can make headings larger (perhaps also using a different font. You might want your book to look more modern, so you could try making your main headings right justified. I would strongly suggest that you don't leave your book exactly as it was in your eBook version, because it will look uninteresting on the page.

On the opposite page are some examples of more adventurous chapter heading styles that you might want to try out.

If you have used Styles (which you should know by now is the way to go with formatting), then all you have to do is modify the style and all of a particular kind of heading will change automatically. Play around with a few styles until you find something that you like, but do this before you continue with your formatting, as changing it later may alter page endings and, if you have formatted your book correctly, you won't want that to happen.

Once you have chosen your Heading Style, go through all your headings and split the long ones up manually with a forced soft return (press Shift and Return together – this will keep the lines together rather than implementing the Paragraph Spacing for the Heading Style). It is usually better for the first line to be slightly longer than the second, but don't split an important phrase in the middle simply to achieve this, as you will lose the flow of the text. See the examples below.

Divide your text like this:

**THINGS TO AVOID WHEN SELF-PUBLISHING YOUR MANUSCRIPT
TO AN EREADER PLATFORM**

rather than splitting 'your' from 'manuscript', like this:

**THINGS TO AVOID WHEN SELF-PUBLISHING YOUR
MANUSCRIPT TO AN EREADER PLATFORM**

Proofreading Checklist

✓ There is only one way to efficiently check headings, no matter which format your book is in – go through all of them one-by-one in a separate pass of your manuscript.

✓ Are all your headings at the correct level? Are they all in the correct font for the level of heading? Are they correctly aligned? Is the capitalisation of the headings consistent and correct?

Chapter One
The Beginning

1

The Beginning

1 The Beginning

Chapter One

THE BEGINNING

- ✓ Make a list (or use your Table of Contents page as a guide) to help check that all are correct and have a section on your style sheet detailing the style of each heading level. If you find something is wrong, check that the correct Heading Style has been selected.
- ✓ If you have used the Table of Contents function to create your contents page and a heading doesn't appear on this list, you have either not updated the Table of Contents before printing, or you haven't assigned the correct Heading Style to the title. Go back and check and then update the Table of Contents.
- ✓ Once your eBook document is converted, flick through it in all the test formats available to ensure that your Headings display correctly, and are readable, in each one. If you find that they are too long, shorten them, unless the only format they appear as too long in is mobile phone format.
- ✓ If headings look like they are oddly spaced across the page, check to see whether or not you might have selected fully justified text for the Heading Style by mistake, but remember, in an eBook this might happen anyway.
- ✓ If you have converted an eBook document to a POD document, you need to be especially careful with the proofreading of your POD document in case you have inadvertently deleted any text around your headings in the process (or changed the format of that text).
- ✓ When you get your POD proof copy back, flick through it just looking at the headings. Do they look like you expected them to? Would they be better if you changed their size? It can be a very different experience looking at something in book format compared to on a printed page or screen. If you have any doubts change them, or ask a friend to take a look. Don't leave something you're not happy with.

FOOTNOTES AND ENDNOTES

I'm sure most of you will know what a footnote is – we're all familiar with seeing an asterisk or a number in the text that relates to a clarification at the bottom of the page – but you may not have heard the term endnote before. It is quite simple really. An endnote is where all the notes are gathered together at the end of a chapter (or possibly a section), rather than at the bottom of a page. The choice between one and the other often depends on how necessary something might be to the reader immediately (ie, in order to understand the text they need to look it up straight away).

eBook

Footnotes and endnotes are rather clumsy in an eBook. If you were to place the notes in the regular place in your document, it might be several pages before a reader came across the note and, by then, they would have forgotten what it related too. Also, if they page forward to find the note, they then have to page back to find their place in the document – a real pain. You could put hyperlinks in, but I still think that results in a clumsy solution.

In addition, you cannot effectively use superscript numbers to mark them. You would simply have to put a bracketed number next to the place where you want to indicate the footnote, which is also rather clumsy.

This is what I do. If I can, I put a clarification in brackets next to the point rather than elsewhere. If I have to separate it out, I put the note immediately below the paragraph it relates to, with an NB to introduce it, in italics. If the reader isn't bothered about the note, they can then simply skip past it. Putting it in italics helps them do this as it is obvious where the note ends.

POD

In a print book your footnotes and endnotes can appear in the traditional place, ie, at the foot of the page or the end of the chapter. However, this will make your book a little more difficult to set out. The automatic Footnote and Endnote function in Microsoft Word is the easiest way to do this.

Both footnotes and endnotes are often in a smaller font size and are separated from the text either by several line spaces, or by a separator line. If you only have one note on a page, or in a chapter, you can use a simple asterisk in the text (immediately next to the word or phrase it relates to) and repeat the asterisk, separated by one space from the note, where it appears. If you have more than one, then you need to use numbers to define them and you need to have them appear as Superscript Text (above the line and in a slightly smaller font size). Obviously, the numbers need to continue in numerical order through the page or chapter.

Proofreading Checklist

✓ If you are using the method I described for putting notes into an eBook, then you simply need to proofread the text as normal as you go through your manuscript.

✓ Proofreading a print book will be a little more complicated. After you have checked the actual text is correct, you need to make sure all the notes appear on the correct page, against the correct footnote number and in the correct order as compared to the text. If you have a lot of footnotes it is very easy to get them in the wrong order. Take extra care over this stage.

HYPERLINKS AND WEB ADDRESSES

Hyperlinks are clickable links in your book that will take you to another page, a website or an eMail address. The print book equivalent is simply writing out the web address or eMail in the text, or referencing the other page.

Obviously, the accuracy of this information is paramount. There is nothing more annoying than clicking on a link, or typing in a web address, and finding that it goes nowhere. In most cases, I would suggest that you only reference the home page of a website, as sub-pages are notorious for being deleted.

eBook

Hyperlinks can be placed in your book either by entering a valid website address and letting Microsoft Word convert it automatically when you press the spacebar (if you have this enabled), or by highlighting a word (or phrase) and adding a hyperlink to it. In general, I think the second method is the best one to use in an eBook because it is cleaner and shorter. Some web addresses can be very long and will not display well on a small eBook screen.

Be careful not to put too many hyperlinks right next to each other in your eBook. This can cause readers problems when they accidentally click on them and are directed away from their reading – very annoying. This is particularly easy to do on touch screens when swiping across to change pages.

If you do have a list of hyperlinks, space them out using Paragraph Spacing, so that even someone on a small touch screen can avoid clicking on the wrong one.

I also think that it is a good idea to warn people that a hyperlink is coming up (even though it should be obvious because they appear as underlined text). A simple phrase like, 'If you want to visit their website, please click here' should be enough. That way, people will be less likely to hit it accidentally. Don't forget that the reader will not always be connected to their

Wi-Fi and accidentally clicking a link will give them an error message.

Hyperlinks can also be used to direct people to other pages in your book. However, there is a potential downside. If the device does not have a back button (or the reader doesn't realise they have one), the reader will be stuck at the new location and have to navigate their way back through the Table of Contents. I would suggest providing a link back to the text they were reading so that this doesn't happen.

Proofreading Checklist

✓ Hyperlinks need to be checked and checked again. First, check that they go to the correct page in your original manuscript and check them once again after you have converted your document in case something goes wrong with the file. It is not only extremely annoying for readers to find that a link doesn't work, it could also harm your future sales if the links are to your other books, your website, your Facebook page or your Twitter account.

POD

In a print book you don't have the luxury of clickable links, so you will have to type out all web addresses and eMail addresses in full. In a print book it is more difficult to update information quickly, so, as I mentioned above, don't reference sub-pages unless you absolutely have to. Constantly changing your print book could be expensive.

Make sure you remove any automatically generated hyperlinks from your print book as the different text colour may look faded in black and white and the underlining could be confusing. It is also possible that the retailer site's conversion software will count it as a full-colour book if these links are highlighted in a different colour in your source document.

Proofreading Checklist

✓ In a print book, you must check that every letter, number, dot, dash and forward slash is written correctly. To be one hundred per cent sure, copy the text into your browser and use it to access the page – if it works, then you know you have typed it in correctly.

GRAPHICS

Graphics, whether they are photographs, illustrations, tables or graphs, can be very useful, especially in a non-fiction book. They break up the text and can help explain concepts much more easily.

They should usually be in jpeg format and inserted into the document by using the Insert Picture Function, not Copy and Paste. You will need to look at the instructions for the particular format to which you are publishing to see what dimensions and dpi (dots per inch) you need to select for your images.

Graphics generally look better when they are centred and with a space top and bottom and they should be placed as close to the reference in the text as space allows.

When looking at the examples below, remember that you don't want to disadvantage readers depending on whether they are able to see the images in colour, black and white or greyscale.

Photographs and Illustrations

When using photographs and illustrations you need to be careful that the colour contrast is good enough to look good in a non-colour format. If you add text to the image, ensure that it stands out and that it is big enough to read.

Look at these two images. What are the good and bad points of each in terms of colour?

I can't show you the actual colour images in the print version of this book, but you can see them at the back of the eBook. For the paperback readers, the colours used are red, yellow and brown for the figures and royal blue for the background on the right-hand picture. The text is in white, black and light blue.

Neither of these two images is perfect, but their purpose is to illustrate potential difficulties. The first one seems a little lacking in contrast as the colours on the figures are in pale watercolours and appear as virtually the same colour in black and white. The illustration also doesn't have a background colour. The second image does have a background colour, which provides some contrast, but which text colour is better? Obviously, not the original, which is black, but would the light blue (bottom centre) give enough contrast? Always check photographs and illustrations in black and white before you commit.

Tables

There are many variations on how tables can be displayed. I have included a few pointers here aimed at helping you to make your tables readable.

The main point I would make is that tables need to lead the eye across properly so people don't get confused as to what items relate to one another. Tables in books tend to have fewer guide lines, so need to be set out as clearly as possible. The easiest way to achieve this is to create your tables in Microsoft Word using the Tables Function and to put all the individual pieces of information into different cells.

Below is an example of a badly displayed table:

	Column 1	Column 2
Category 1	Description of first category split over two lines	
		Description of first category
Category 2		Particularly long description of second category that splits over four lines...
	Description of second category	In two sections
Category 3	Description of third category	
		Description of third category

Even though the categories don't overlap each other, where a section starts and ends is not clear. The information would be better displayed as in this next example:

	Column 1	Column 2
Category 1	Description of first category split over two lines	Description of first category
Category 2	Description of second category	Particularly long description of second category that splits over four lines...
		In two sections
Category 3	Description of third category	Description of third category

Even though there are no physical lines drawn on the page, the eye can easily read across the lines of text.

If you have a table with figures, the numbers must line up to the visible (or invisible) decimal point. You will need to have defined your style for this in your style sheet. Let's look at some examples.

	Column 1	Column 2
Category 1	1	4
Category 2	3.5	2.73
Category 3	5600	365
Category 4	91.33	42.1

In this first table, all the numbers are left-aligned as they would appear in an unformatted document. Many people, at this point, would align them all to the right or centre them. This is incorrect.

	Column 1	Column 2
Category 1	1	4
Category 2	3.5	2.73
Category 3	5600	365
Category 4	91.33	42.1

This second example shows all the figures aligned to the decimal point, but it looks uneven because they aren't all showing figures after the decimal point. Some house styles would leave it like this because the numbers themselves are not comparable, but they are now more easily read because of the alignment.

	Column 1	Column 2
Category 1	1.00	4.00
Category 2	3.50	2.73
Category 3	5600.00	365.00
Category 4	91.33	42.10

This final example shows all the figures aligned to the decimal point, but they have been evened out, ie, they have an equal number of zeros after the decimal point. This is more visually pleasing to the eye.

Choose the format that works best for the numbers you have to display.

Numbers will have to be very carefully checked for accuracy. Even if you have taken the table from a spreadsheet you should double-check them all and any calculations that have been made.

Graphs

The main thing to remember about using graphs, apart from them being large enough to read, is to make them understandable in a non-colour format. That means that you often can't simply use colours to define the items in your key. Compare these three examples of the same graph:

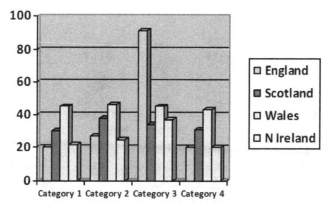

This first example above uses Microsoft Word's default settings. All the colours are very similar, the graph is 3D and it has a background. None of these will be helpful to someone with a black and white display. It is very difficult to work out which column is Wales and which one is Northern Ireland and yet, in colour, the original light yellow and pale blue are very different.

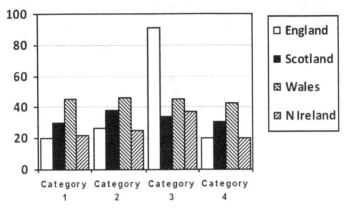

Compare it to the second one. What I have done here is to change the column fills to simple patterns using only black and white, removed the background colour, removed the 3D effect, knocked back the colour of the guide lines to a light grey and increased the width of the columns. Even having done that, when the graphic is viewed on a small screen, it is still difficult to determine which one is Wales and which Northern Ireland.

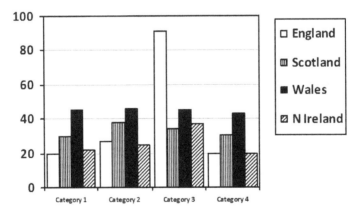

In this final example, the patterned columns have been split from each other with the solid block of black between them, and vertical lines and diagonal lines have been used as fills, rather than two variations of diagonal lines. When creating something like this, you will need to play around with the settings and test it in black and white before finalising, but I hope these examples have given you food for thought.

Even with a graph consisting of lines you can have different line formats, such as, solid, thick solid, even dashes, uneven dashes and dots, to differentiate between them in black and white.

eBook

All the items I have discussed in this section need to be imported as a picture into your document to work in eBook format. Forget the fact that you can create tables and graphs directly into the document – they won't work properly, if at all. I found the best way to do this was to use the print screen option on my keyboard in the original document and to transfer them to a drawing package in order to save them as a .jpeg, before importing them back into Microsoft Word. The resolution of the images isn't as high as a photographic image, but is adequate for most eReaders.

There are several things you need to consider when placing graphics into an eBook. They make it into a larger file, they can be difficult to read and they can make your file a little more complex to convert. Also, if you are uploading to Kindle Direct Publishing (KDP), there are charges for downloading files depending on the file size and these are taken off your profits. The larger the file = the less profit you will make.

If you don't absolutely need them, and can get the information across in a different way, I would suggest that you try to avoid them.

For example, when I first wrote the section about punctuation, I included a graphic showing the difference between plain punctuation and italicised punctuation. Then it occurred to me that I could do exactly the same thing in the text by simply enlarging the punctuation symbols. Formatting with an eBook is sometimes about thinking creatively and coming up with different solutions rather than blindly following what you would do in a print copy.

When using graphics in an eBook, placement is much easier than in a print copy. You can put them right next to the reference in the text, but never choose the option to have the text wrap around them – this will not work. It might be a good idea to put page breaks either side of a graphic if it is large, so that it will always have its own page.

If you do put your graphics on a separate page, I would suggest you put a line at the end of the previous text saying something like, 'See graphic on next page', because the page ending might look a little odd and this will explain to the reader why that is.

If you do use graphics, please make sure that you view them on an actual eReader before you publish. If they provide a bad reading experience, your readers will not be impressed.

POD

When placing graphics into a print book you have much more flexibility in how they look.

You can have text wrap around your graphics rather than having them stand alone in the centre of the page (although this is the normal way to display them – wraparound text is more common in newsletters than books). If necessary, you can turn them sideways (landscape) and it won't be confusing to the reader. You also have more flexibility in terms of naming them and possibly numbering them.

Place your graphics as close to the mention in the text as possible, but you will have to consider how they fit on the page, depending on the size they need to be and how much space is left. The opposite page, or even over the page is good enough as long as everything is properly referenced and numbered (in the text as well as on the graphic).

Once again, be careful with the use of colour. A full-colour book will cost a lot more to produce than a black and white book. This may not be an issue if your topic warrants the cost being passed on to the purchaser, but it could reduce your profits significantly.

Proofreading Checklist

✓ Depending on the graphic concerned, proofreading can pose a number of problems. If you do use graphics that contain words or numbers, eg, a children's book or a spreadsheet, don't forget to print these out and proofread them properly as well in a separate pass of your manuscript.

✓ When you have converted your eBook version, make sure that the graphic is readable on the normal-sized screen. Has the image degraded? Does the text need to be bigger. Is it actually going to work in an eBook?

✓ If your graphics really don't work well in your eBook, you could possibly have a link to a website with the graphics available there.

✓ In your POD proof, make sure that the graphics are close enough to the text to make sense when you read the book. Make sure they can be read without difficulty – it can be easy to think something is big enough on a screen, but when you get your proof back, it can look very different.

✓ Check, double-check and triple check any figures and calculations.

FORMS AND TO DO LISTS

These can be useful in an instruction book. They leave a space in the book for the reader to note down important information from what they have learned so far, and are frequently used.

Make sure that you leave enough space for someone with normal handwriting to fill in the necessary information.

eBook

I'm hoping that I don't need to tell you that these don't work in an eBook. People cannot write in your eBook in the same way they can in a print copy.

I actually downloaded a non-fiction eBook a while back that fell into this trap. After every chapter or section there were spaces left for you to fill in information. Yes, there was a one, two, three, etc, in the eBook, just as there would have been in the print copy. All they needed to have done was removed those sections and put something along the lines of, 'Take a piece of paper and write down ... ' – it wouldn't have been difficult to do while they were formatting the book.

If you are converting an eBook from an old paper document, remember to rethink instructions. You don't want to look like you're not interested in your digital reading audience and that book certainly felt like that to me.

(*NB: Some eReaders now have a facility to print out pages, which could be useful for forms. However, there is usually a limit per book or author, for copyright reasons, so it might not be the best solution.*)

POD

Likewise, if you've created your eBook and are converting it to a paper version, maybe you could insert those lists or forms.

And one final thought on this. If you really do want to provide structured forms or lists for people to fill out, why not create a website for them and link to it in your book? Often people don't want to write in books, even if they can. But if you take this route, make sure you proofread everything you are asking people to download and provide it as a .pdf file so that the maximum number of people possible can access the information.

Proofreading Checklist

✓ Is the list or form appropriate for the format?

✓ Is there enough space for people to write? Try writing in it yourself in your normal handwriting.

PAGE NUMBERS

Page numbers can be formatted in many different ways (header or footer, centred or outside edge, plain text or italics, etc), but there are a few conventions you have to remember when using them, as follows:

- Left-hand pages are even and right-hand pages are odd numbers;
- All pages are counted in the numbering, but not actually numbered until after the copyright page;
- The front matter is usually numbered with small Roman numerals, centred at the bottom of the page;
- The main text is numbered with Arabic numerals and always starts on a right-hand page (ie, the odd-numbered page, Page 1). The back matter is numbered continuously after the main text in Arabic numerals.

eBook

Numbering is not usually possible in eBooks. All eBooks have an estimated number of pages, but that is a calculation done on word count, unless you also have a print version linked to your eBook, in which case the number of pages in the paperback might be quoted.

You must never put numbers into your document when you create it as this will cause problems with your converted document.

POD

Print books, of course, must be numbered. Chose your style, positioning and size, and place your numbers into your document Header or Footer. Look at books in your genre/subject to see what is the most common style.

To have different numbering systems for front matter and main text you will need to insert Section Breaks or use one of the pre-formatted book templates from the POD publisher.

Proofreading Checklist

✓ With regards to proofreading your numbers, your Microsoft Word document, when set-up properly into sections, should be okay – a computer won't miss out a number by mistake. However, the printing process could be flawed, so when you get your proof copy back from your POD service, start by checking the numbers to ensure that all the pages have been printed and bound correctly. If the numbering isn't correct, it is likely that your proof copy is faulty and you will need to get a correct copy before you can start checking it properly.

?

There is a spelling mistake in the POD section above. Did you spot it? Look for a single letter that should be a double.

RUNNING HEAD(LINES)

Running headlines (often called running heads) are the headers across the top of the page that you frequently see in a print book.

These repeat the chapter headings, sub-headings and the title of the book or the author's name, depending on the style used. There are two basic conventions as far as layout is concerned (although house styles may vary):

- In a fiction book you will usually find the book title on the left-hand side and the chapter title or author on the right-hand side.
- In a non-fiction book you might see the above, but could also see the chapter title on the left-hand side and the relevant sub-title (ie, the one that appears on the page below, or the most recent on the previous pages) on the right-hand side.
- You will not usually have a headline on the first page of a chapter. This can only be achieved by putting a section break at the beginning of each chapter and creating a Different First Page for each. If you use the POD template, this should be set for you.

eBook

As with numbers, you cannot use running headlines in an eBook. There is nowhere for them to go. The eReader has its own headers and footers. If you have them in your document you must remove them.

POD

Unless you are a real expert with Section Breaks and Headers, always use a publisher's template to format your print book. Choose your style (as above) and go through each section (chapter) and change the text in the template – you will only need to do this once in each section. You could use a smaller font for your headlines so that they aren't too intrusive.

In the print version of this book I chose to put the author name on the left-hand page and the chapter title on the right-hand page. This is because, when you flick through a book, your eye is drawn more to the right-hand page and I felt it was more useful to see the chapter title than my name.

Proofreading Checklist

✓ Take extra care with checking the text in your running headlines, if something is incorrect, the error could appear on as many as half the pages in your book.

✓ When you get your POD proof back, do a separate pass to ensure all your running headlines are correct. You won't need to check the detail of the text on every single page, but you will need to make sure that the correct headline is in the correct place in each chapter.

USING FIND AND REPLACE

I have mentioned several times in the previous sections about the possibility of using the Find and Replace Function to highlight errors and correct them. This advice comes with a BIG WARNING.

Before you use Find and Replace, make sure you check the 'full word only' option in your software. You may not think what you are searching for could be included in another word, but you'd be surprised. I once did it to replace the name Chris in a story about Christmas – yes, you got it. I realised before sending the story out, but there are many less obvious examples that might not jump out at you. What if I had been changing the name Paul to something else and the story was about camping? There would likely have been a reference to a tarpaulin in there somewhere.

I have also talked about using Find and Replace for formatting. I wouldn't suggest using it for anything too complex, but in addition to the double spaces I discussed, you could also search for text formatted in a different colour, for example. This might be useful if you were to test displaying your book as white text on black. If you found that your text was invisible in some places, you could search for black text and replace it with automatic (although the better option would be to ensure it was formatted to Normal Style, which should already be set to automatic).

To access the formatting options you need to click on Advanced or More list (depending on the version of Microsoft Word that you have) in the pop-up window and select the appropriate function.

SANDIE GILES

COVERS

Most of what I'm going to say here will assume that you are creating your own cover. However, you should also bear these things in mind if you are commissioning a cover from a professional. One would hope that they would know what is necessary to make an eBook cover stand out and be readable in the online market, but that may not be the case.

So, what do you need on your cover?

An image that will draw people in, the title of the book and the author are absolute musts. Some book covers also have a notable review (a few words only), a sub-title, or another graphic (such as a star) to encompass a short description of an important element of the book's content.

What you must remember is that when you sell online, everything needs to be bigger and brighter. The reason for this is that people will only ever see your cover image in a thumbnail, or much reduced size to the actual cover, until they decide to click on your book. If they are to be enticed to take that step, they need to be able to understand the genre and read the title.

A very dark image is generally bad. A very thin font is generally bad.

Look at the covers for other authors in your genre – if your cover doesn't conform to what people expect, they might not give yours a chance.

The only way you can test the cover you have created is to reduce the size down to the same size you would see on a retailer website.

What can you see? What can't you see? What about if there was a bit of glare on the screen as you were looking at it? Would it still stand out?

There are various theories on how many seconds it takes for someone to decide whether or not to investigate a book further – anything from five upwards to a very generous ten or fifteen. Five seconds isn't very long. If someone has to squint at your cover to see what it is, they probably won't bother. So, make it stand out and make sure there are absolutely no errors.

eBook

Different eBook conversions have different requirements for image size, but these should be easily found on the relevant website. Don't create anything that doesn't conform to normal sizing because it will make your book stand out as self-published in a bad way (eg, a landscape cover instead of portrait – unless it's a children's picture book). What is to stop people thinking, 'Well, if they can't even get the cover right ... " and passing on your book immediately?

Don't put the cover image into your file unless the instructions tell you to. Covers are usually uploaded separately and integrated by the retailer. If you put it into the document as well, there might be two images in your book.

POD

The cover on a POD book is much more complex than for an eBook. Obviously, you will want to use the same image on the front for customer recognition, but it is no longer a simple page-sized image with your title and author name. A print book needs a front cover, a back cover and a spine. It could be worth using a proper cover designer to get this right.

If you decide to go it alone, most POD publishers will have a template formatting section for covers, but you do need to have made the decisions on how you want it to look before you start to create your cover.

Do you want your cover picture to extend all the way around your book? Will you repeat the same image front and back? Will the back cover be a plain colour? Once again, I would suggest that you look at books in your genre and see what traditional publishers do. The easiest option would be to use the front cover as is and make the back cover the same background colour as the front, but this might not be right for your genre.

Of course, the back cover also needs text and the format is, I think, one of the least standard parts of a book. The one thing it absolutely must have is a barcode (this will be provided by the POD service, but you will probably have to paste it on to the background image or leave a space clear). The barcode is important because it contains pricing and ISBN information for potential sellers. There are also requirements regarding sizing and placement of such barcodes – make sure you read the instructions on this carefully before finalising your cover.

Other than that, the back cover is your canvas to paint as you wish. Things that you will often see on traditionally published books, and you might want to include on yours, are:

- A brief synopsis of the book;
- An author bio (and picture);
- Review quotes.

You may be able to use the synopsis (blurb) you use on retailer sites for this, but I would suggest that you make it as concise as possible so as not to crowd the page. It is fairly standard to use fully justified text, ie, straight left-hand and straight right-hand margins, with no indents.

If you do decide to put an author bio on the back (rather than inside), you should make it very brief. Two or three sentences are more than enough and any picture should be small. The synopsis is much more important – make sure that stands out.

Using review quotes is a tricky one. Firstly, the quotes have to be worth-while. It's no good quoting your best friend's opinion, that isn't going to pull the readers in. Quotes are only really effective if they are from recog-nised publications, experts in the field, or well-known authors. Before put-ting any quotes on the cover (or inside the book, for that matter), make sure you have permission to reproduce them and that you reproduce them in the way they were originally intended. Quotes are usually centred and often in italics (and don't forget the quotation marks).

When formatting the text, don't use more than a couple of different fonts and make sure they are readable – script fonts are bad for the majority of people to read, but italics, in a basic font, can be effective as a highlighter. However, if you are putting text on a coloured background you need to make sure that it stands out well enough. White text on a black background might need to be a little bigger to be readable and text colours like bright pinks and purples don't work well. Black text on a grey background might also disappear. Not everyone has good eyesight or the correct glasses. Use common sense and try printing the cover out before you finalise it. Your printer version won't give an exact representation of a properly printed cover, but it won't be too far out.

Proofreading Checklist

✓ You cannot have any text errors on your cover. Would you buy a book by an author you didn't know if there was a spelling mistake and a missing word on the back copy? Check it fifty times if you have to, but make sure it is one hundred per cent correct. There aren't very many words on a front cover, so it's easy to just glance at one and think it is correct. Don't fall into this trap and don't assume that because you have had your cover prepared by a professional that it is error-free. Keep in mind that, you are so familiar with the title of your book and the spelling of your own name, it would be easy to gloss over any errors.

✓ Once you have made sure that the words are correct. Then, make sure that the capitalisation is correct – you can find the rules for this under Headings.

FRONT MATTER? BACK MATTER?

Now you have come to the point where you need to decide what you are going to include in the front matter of your book and what will appear as back matter.

Front matter is the pages that appear at the front of the book before the main text. Back matter is everything that appears after the main text at the back of the book.

The amount of pages you create in your front matter will affect the formatting of the rest of the book, so decide on what you are including and stick to it. Whether you are creating an eBook or a print book, you must consider what text will be available in the sample or Look Inside on the retailer website. If your book is less than novel length, having a lot of front matter could affect how effective this useful marketing tool is.

The text in your front and back matter needs to be displayed well. You should take as much care over this as with your main text.

Below are the things that either must, or can, be included in your front or back matter – don't think that you have to include everything. Only add the items that are relevant to your book. They are listed here in the order they usually appear, although there may be slight variations according to a publisher's house style.

TITLE PAGE

The title page is simply what it sounds like – a page where the only information is the title of the book, the author and the publisher. Some books also have a half title page before the title page that only has the book title.

eBook

I would argue that a title page (or half title page) is not relevant in an eBook. People already have the title on the cover within their downloaded file and it can be included on the copyright page as well. It adds nothing except extra file size and pages to skip through and it will reduce the amount of main text available in your book sample, but not by a huge amount. You may also find that people don't even see it in the downloaded book, because the start page for the document (ie, where the book opens after you have downloaded it), is beyond that point.

POD

In a print book, the title page always appears on the first right-hand page (or if you have a half title page, the second right-hand page). The text is centred across the page and spaced slightly above the centre line. The text can be bold and large – but not too large. You don't want your main title taking up more than two lines.

You don't have to worry about using line returns to space down the page here, although using Paragraph Spacing would be better, as your book will be saved as a .pdf file for printing and spacing will be fixed.

It would be unusual not to have a title page in a print book, so you should definitely include one.

Proofreading Checklist

✔ This is the first page in your book. Even though many people may skip through it, it must be correct. Be aware that, as with your cover, you are so familiar with the title of the book, and your own name, that it is easy to make mistakes. Don't assume you will have got it correct.

COPYRIGHT PAGE

The copyright page is essential to make your book look professional, although it is not strictly necessary – works are protected by copyright as soon as you have written them – but people expect to see a copyright page in your book and it doesn't simply contain your copyright statement.

Copyright pages are usually set out as follows:

- The title of your book and author name (optional);
- A copyright statement that should, at the very least, contain the word Copyright, the copyright symbol (if your publishing platform supports the Special Character), the year of copyright and your name as the copyright holder, but will usually also include a statement about not copying the contents;

- A standard disclaimer about your characters being from your imagination, etc, for fiction;
- An ISBN number if you have one;
- Publisher details, if relevant;
- Edition details, if relevant;
- Cover illustrator or designer details, if relevant;
- Editor, if relevant.

There are many different forms of copyright statement and disclaimer – read through the ones in the books you have on your shelf and decide on a wording that you are comfortable with, but only copy it if you are sure it is not individual to the author or publisher (ie, they have the copyright for it).

Text on a copyright page is usually centred and a normal font size (or slightly smaller), apart from the book title and author, which can be larger and emboldened text.

eBook

There are many people who will advise that your copyright page is not something that should be at the beginning of an eBook and advocate putting it into the back matter instead. I disagree.

One of the issues with self-published eBooks is that the potential customer may perceive them, rightly or wrongly, as unprofessional and slapdash. A copyright page makes the book look professional. I would leave it at the front.

If the length of your book isn't long enough to cope with this as front matter and still have a decent Look Inside or sample, I would suggest that your book might not be long enough to justify selling it. There are exceptions to this, of course, such as poetry and flash fiction collections, which tend to have fewer words than other books.

POD

The copyright page usually appears on the back of the title page, although it can appear on a right-hand page, depending on house style.

Space the text out evenly down the page. Don't leave it all squashed at the top. Some styles leave the text in the bottom half of the page, but it still needs to be properly spaced out.

Proofreading Checklist

✔ Check all the information on this page very carefully. It is extremely important that your ISBN number is correct, for example, as this is the catalogue number for your book.

✔ If you use a copyright symbol in your eBook, make sure that it converts properly, otherwise just use the word Copyright on its own.

(TABLE OF) CONTENTS PAGE

A contents page (or table of contents) contains a list of chapters, and possibly sub-sections, in your book. In an eBook it will be a clickable list and in a print book it will be referenced with page numbers.

A contents page in a non-fiction book may be used by a potential purchaser to see if it contains the information they are looking for. Make sure your titles are clear – sometimes being too clever with your titles can be detrimental to your sales.

eBook

A contents page can take up a lot of space at the front of your book. If you are writing a novel, seriously consider whether or not you need one, especially if your chapter headings are simply Chapter 1, 2, 3, etc. People will be reading your book from beginning to end, not jumping about through chapters and eReaders generally bookmark your last page read, so they are not needed for that purpose. If the retailer requires one, consider using it to simply mark the start of the book, acknowledgements, author page, etc, to reduce the length.

Short story and poetry collections definitely need a contents page. If you haven't mentioned in your book blurb how many pieces are in the book, a potential reader can see the number at a glance before they buy – and they might find the titles intriguing.

Non-fiction books should always have a contents page for the reason described above. However, non-fiction contents pages can be long. You must make sure that yours doesn't take up the entire sample of the book. Maybe only include the chapter headings or one level of sub-heading to condense it a little if this is an issue.

POD

It is rare to see a print book without a contents page and it usually starts on a right-hand page. Make sure that the it is formatted and in place so that you know how many pages it is going to take up. If you are using the automatic Table of Contents Function it will capture the page numbers for you, but remember you will have to go back right at the end of your formatting and update the page numbers in case something has changed during the process.

There are many different styles used for these pages. Some have leader dots between the heading and the number to guide your eyes across (useful if you have a very detailed contents page). Some have sub-headings indented and others just keep them at the margin, but maybe in a different font. Choose whatever looks best for your particular publication.

Proofreading Checklist

✓ If you've chosen to use the Table of Contents Function, you won't have to proofread the text separately, you will have done this already by proofreading the main text, but you must make sure that all the headings appear – if they don't you didn't update it after your final changes or one of your headings isn't in a proper Heading Style. However, having said that you don't *need* to proofread the Table of Contents, it can sometimes be a good way to help isolate your headings for proofreading.

✓ Use your contents page as one final check to see if your headings make sense and are not too long, or even if you might want to change the order of chapters in a non-fiction book.

DEDICATION

If you have a dedication you want to include in your book (these are usually only a couple of sentences long), I would always put it in the front, because a dedication is about and for someone who means a lot to you. Why hide that at the back? Dedications are often centred and sometimes in italics.

eBook

Put the dedication right at the top of the page and put another page break immediately after it.

POD

Dedications can be set out much more pleasingly in a print book. As with the Title Page, place the text just above the centre of the page for the best effect. They usually appear on a right-hand page, but can sometimes be seen on a left-hand page.

Proofreading Checklist

✔ No special tips for proofreading here, other than checking the text carefully. I recently saw a dedication in a book where the author was thanking their spouse for putting up with them, except the word 'with' never made it into the book. It is very easily done.

FOREWORD

A foreword is a piece written by another author or an expert on the subject you are covering in your book. It will be attributed to them and usually dated. The length varies, from a single paragraph, to a piece several pages long.

eBook and POD

You should seriously consider whether you need this in the front of your book as every little thing that increases the front matter and reduces the sample of your work is potentially damaging your sales. If it isn't a big selling point for your book that this person has contributed, you might be better using their contribution in some other way (see Afterword).

If you do use one, set it out in the same way as a chapter, with the contributor's name and the date right-aligned at the bottom of the text and maybe differentiated by using italics.

POD

The foreword should start on a right-hand page.

Proofreading Checklist

✔ As this piece has been written by someone else, if you want to change anything, you will need to liaise with them directly. On the one hand, you don't want spelling or grammatical errors in your book, on the other, you don't want to upset your contributor.

PREFACE

A preface is usually there to inform people about how you came to write the book. Once again, it could be a simple paragraph, or several pages long.

eBook and POD

I would strongly suggest that, unless the piece is very short, if you want people to have this information, you should publish it as a blog post or an article instead. Putting this in your front matter might not help to sell your book and it reduces the sample text available. There are also places on some retailer websites where you can put a piece from the author – could this information go there instead? If you feel you absolutely have to have one and do include it, make sure that it entices people to buy.

POD

A preface should be set out like a chapter and start on a right-hand page.

Proofreading Checklist

✓ Get someone else to read this piece and to be honest with you about whether it adds to the book.
✓ Proofread as for main text.

ACKNOWLEDGEMENTS

Many people like to add acknowledgements to their book. It means they can officially thank everyone who helped in its production, which is a good thing. Have a sheet of paper with your manuscript documents where you can keep a note of all the people you want to include.

Acknowledgements usually also include family members, friends and people who have inspired the author.

Personally, I think brief is best. I might glance over the names if they are half a page, but anything more and I swiftly turn the page. However, the acknowledgements aren't really for the reader, so it's up to you.

Do break it up into paragraphs so that the text doesn't look like one great big block and add a few words of explanation as to why the names are there. You never know, if you highlight that a particular person was your editor, they might get future business from it.

Although acknowledgements are sometimes in the front matter in a traditional print book, I would suggest putting them in the back matter for a self-published book. This is quite common in print books as well, so people won't think it's strange.

eBook

I would keep acknowledgements as brief as possible in an eBook. Although they can be set out to look good in a print book, in an eBook three pages worth of names listed one after the other is not attractive and people might simply close the eBook there.

POD

Acknowledgements should start on a right-hand page. Sometimes the text is centred, although I think left-aligned looks more professional.

Proofreading Checklist

- ✓ Make absolutely sure you have all the names spelled correctly (you don't want to offend people). If necessary, ask them to e-mail you with their name exactly as they would like it to appear.
- ✓ When proofreading, read one name at a time – block the next one out with your thumb. Check the capitalisation carefully and, don't forget to keep the punctuation consistent, ie, if you're not using full stops for abbreviations, then don't let them slip into names.

INTRODUCTION OR PROLOGUE

Introductions are usually found in non-fiction books and prologues in fiction books, but they serve basically the same purpose. They set the scene for what is to come.

In an introduction, that might be the kinds of things included in the book and how you intend to tackle them, in a prologue it might be some of the back story to the novel. Make sure that the text adds to what comes next and is relevant. An introduction can be useful to a potential purchaser as they can see how the information is to be presented and what it will include. Prologues, on the other hand, are reportedly often skipped by readers.

Set the text out as you would for a chapter.

POD

Start this section on a right-hand page.

Proofreading Checklist

- ✓ Proofread as for body text.

HALF TITLE

If you have used a lot of the front matter items in your book, you might want to insert a(nother) half title page to indicate that this is where the main text of the book starts.

Centre the text in a larger, emboldened font.

POD

The half title page should be on a right-hand page with the text just above the half-way mark.

Proofreading Checklist

✔ Once again, don't assume that just because this is only a title that there couldn't possibly be a mistake in it.

CONCLUSION OR EPILOGUE

Now we're on to the things that are usually placed in the back matter of your book, ie, everything that comes after the main text.

Similar to the introduction or prologue, the conclusion or epilogue sums-up a piece, the first being the form for a non-fiction book, the second being for fiction. The conclusion will pick out the important points and summarise them, whereas the epilogue might tell you what has happened to the characters a few years on from the story (in brief).

Format them in the same way as your chapter text.

POD

Start on a right-hand page in your print book.

Proofreading Checklist

✔ Proofread as for main text.

AFTERWORD

An afterword is sometimes included in non-fiction books. In the same way as the foreword, it is usually written by someone else and sums up the book in relation to the subject. Set the afterword out in the same way as a chapter and include the author's name and the date, possibly right-aligned, at the end of the text.

Consider whether you could use an afterword instead of a foreword in your book, to reduce the front matter.

POD

Set your afterword to start on a right-hand page.

Proofreading Checklist

✓ As with the foreword, consider the implications of any changes that need to be made to the text.

APPENDICES

Appendices are generally used to collect information together that is useful to the reader, but would clutter up the main text. They might include further clarification on a subject or lists of information. As the types of things that can be included in your appendices, or separately if you prefer, are in the items below, I will discuss them separately, but they might include:

* A reading list;
* Useful organisations, websites, etc;
* Answers to exercises in the book;
* Your author profile.

Start each new appendix on a new page.

POD

The first appendix will usually start on a right-hand page, but subsequent ones might continue on a left-hand page.

GLOSSARY

If your book is non-fiction and technical, I would suggest that a glossary could be useful to your readers. It is used to provide an alphabetical list of definitions for terms that people might not understand. Pay particular attention to making sure that your glossary entries are clear and concise, otherwise there is no point in having them – try getting someone who does not know the subject to read through them and see if they understand what you are trying to say. Think about your audience when compiling the list. Your readers may have varying levels of knowledge and competence. Don't assume that they will all understand the simpler terms.

Try keeping a piece of paper beside you as you write to note down potential glossary entries – if you don't you'll have to do a separate pass on your manuscript after you finish writing.

eBook

Think about how you lay your glossary out so that it is easily readable on a screen and test out formats on your converted document, for example:

Glossary – A glossary contains a list of technical terms in a book that may need further explanation.

or

Glossary
A glossary contains a list of technical terms in a book that may need further explanation.

Which one do you think is easier to read in eBook format? Don't forget that not all eReaders display the text in the same way. Test your layout in all formats.

POD

As emboldening in a print book is easier to see, a simple list format might work well for your glossary. It will also take up less space and paper. You might also consider using a multiple column format.

A glossary will usually start on a right-hand page.

Proofreading Checklist

✓ Make sure the list is easy to read.
✓ Check that a layman is able to understand your explanations.

FURTHER READING OR BIBLIOGRAPHY

These are only relevant for a non-fiction book.

A further reading list should contain any reference materials you consider relevant to the people who buy your book.

A bibliography is more likely to contain books that have been referenced in the text and that may have provided inspiration for the book – although it can just be a reading list.

Formal book references normally contain the following information (but the order may vary), although the last two items are often omitted:

- Book title;
- Author name (generally surname followed by initials);
- Publisher;
- Location (ie, where the book was published);
- Year of publication;

These items usually appear on a single line, separated by commas. The book title is normally italicised.

A magazine reference will typically include:

- The title of the article;
- The volume (edition number);
- The page number;
- The date published;
- The publisher (often omitted).

If you are referencing an online publication, you will need to adapt this a little. It will probably have a publication date that you can add (if it is displayed like an actual magazine), or a posting date.

eBook

Although you could use the same conventions of display as for a print book, I think this information is more easily digested if displayed in a different way.

For example, a traditional format might look like this:

Really Good Book, with a sub-title, Author, E, The Publishing House, London, 2013

On an eBook this simply looks like a mass of text when there are multiple entries, partly because a print book would usually use hanging paragraphs and those don't work well in eBooks. Whereas, if you display the information by separating it onto different lines, it could look like this:

Really Good Book with a sub-title
Excellent Author, The Publishing House, London, 2013

This will make it easier to focus on the title of the book. It may take up a few more pages to do it this way, but there will be no increase in words. You have probably noticed that I put the author's name with the surname last – I just think this is easier to read on a small screen and less confusing. I would also be inclined to use bold for the book title, rather than the traditional italics, so that it looks like this:

Really Good Book with a sub-title
Excellent Author, The Publishing House, London, 2013

If you can, add a hyperlink to the book at the retailer you are publishing with, so that people can easily find it.

POD

When you create your reading list in your POD book, I would use the traditional format, because you don't want to take up more space than necessary, otherwise you will increase the cost of your book. Therefore, have the information displayed on a single line, separated by commas. Set the format to be a hanging paragraph, so that the first line is at the margin and subsequent lines are indented. This will make it easier to see individual titles. For example:

> *Really Good Book*, with a sub-title, Author, E, The Publishing House, London, 2013

This section will usually start on a right-hand page. The text is often smaller than the body text of the book.

Proofreading Checklist

- ✔ These types of lists can be difficult to proofread, especially if the list is long. Your eyes will find difficulty focussing on all the small writing, commas, full stops, etc. I would suggest proofreading this when you are fresh for the day.
- ✔ Make sure all the information is completely correct. You may have a link in an eBook, but in a POD book your reader is relying on what you have written to find that book.
- ✔ Make sure that the capitalisation is the same as on the actual book, even if it doesn't follow the rules you have set for your publication.

OTHER USEFUL INFORMATION

Many non-fiction books will have lists of further information that might be useful to the reader, such as websites, organisations, etc.

For organisations you will need to, at the very least, include their full name, and any abbreviations of this. You might also want to include their address and their contact details, eg, telephone, eMail and website, where relevant. I would also include a couple of lines of explanation as to why they are relevant to the reader, ie, what they do. Think about how you can set this information out clearly (refer back to the sections entitled Glossary and Reading Lists and Bibliographies for ideas).

eBook

If the organisation has a website, make sure you link to it, but I would suggest that you link to the main (home) page rather than a sub-page as these can often change and then the link won't work. Although it is easy to update links and upload a new version of your book if they do change, you won't always know that this has happened.

POD

Try and ensure that the information you give will not go out-of-date too quickly. It isn't as easy to update a print book if information goes out-of-date, as you might have to order another proof copy before you finalise it.

These sections usually start on a right-hand page.

Proofreading Checklist

✔ As well as checking all the information carefully, you must check the links in your eBook version before and after conversion and test the addresses in your POD version by copying them to your browser.
✔ Go through the information once every six months after publication to make sure it is current. Change it and re-upload your book if it isn't.

ABOUT THE AUTHOR(S)

Writing a piece about yourself is always difficult, but this is one of the most important sections of your book – you need to get it right. You want to give people enough information that they trust you to have written a good book, but not so gushing that they think you are overinflating your importance. You also don't want to give them so much that they have no interest in visiting your website to find out more. They are usually written in third person.

Beneath your paragraphs of text, include the address of your website, blog, Facebook page, Twitter account and any other social media presence you may have. Some people also add their eMail address. Personally, I wouldn't, as this could lead to spamming, but if you do, make sure it is a professional looking address and not the one you use for your personal eMails.

If more than one person was involved in writing the book, you will need to include all this information for each person. You might want to change the title of this section to (List of) Contributors or something similar.

eBook

Always place your Author Page in the back matter of an eBook, unless you need to emphasise your qualifications (eg, your first book as a non-fiction expert), although I think this can be more effectively done by combining the information on the retailer's website alongside your blurb.

Make sure that you include hyperlinks to all your website and social media details and, if you are confident about inserting images into your file, why not include an author picture as well? Make the links look attractive, as previously discussed.

POD

Your author information in the POD version of your book can go in a number of places. Some books have them in the front matter, some in the back matter and you will often find a couple of sentences on the back cover. You need to decide what works best for you.

The only difference between the content of your eBook and POD Author Page is that your website and social media links will not be clickable. So, try to make them as short as possible.

If you do decide to put a short bio on the back cover of your book, don't take up too much space. A couple of sentences and a small picture are usually enough. Use that space for more important things, like the description of your book, and have a proper author page inside.

This section will usually start on a right-hand page, but there is no need to start each individual author on a new right-hand page for multiple author publications, although I would suggest a separate page for each one.

Proofreading Checklist

✓ Don't forget, these links are some of the most important ones in your eBook. Check, double-check and triple-check that all your links work.
✓ For your print copy, check that the links work by pasting them into your browser.
✓ Make sure that you don't slip from first person to third person (or vice versa) in your bio. Third person is usually considered better.
✓ If you have multiple contributors, make sure their bios are all written in the same person (first or third).

OTHER PUBLICATIONS BY THE AUTHOR(S)

Sometimes this appears in the front matter, sometimes in the back matter – I prefer the latter. If you decide to put them at the front, I would only put very brief details of your other books – a three line description maybe. Readers want to get to the content at that stage. They don't yet know whether they are interested in reading your other books (which is why I would put it at the back).

Titles and author details are often centred and bold and are followed by the official blurb for the book. Don't include prices, as these often change.

eBook

In an eBook this should definitely go in the back matter.

Advertising your other publications in your eBook is becoming a heavily used marketing technique. Some books have whole chapters of other books tagged onto the end. Personally, I don't like this all that much and I know I'm not the only one. If I have enjoyed the book enough to want to look at the other books, I have already bought into the author's style and story-telling (or for a non-fiction book, their expertise). I also object to a book that, on the face of it, is a couple of hundred pages long, but when you get down to it, fifty or more pages of that is another book chapter or excessive advertising.

The alternative is to simply put the title of the book and the blurb and you might want to link to the book at the same retailer.

POD

In a print book it is more sensible to only include a blurb, not a chapter, otherwise you will be greatly increasing the price of the book to the purchaser. Although the first one will usually be on a right-hand page, you don't necessarily need to start each book on a new page, unless your blurbs are quite long. Obviously, there are no links available in print books, so something like 'Available at all major online retailers' might be appropriate.

Centre the titles and make them larger than you would in an eBook.

Proofreading Checklist

- ✓ Double-check all links by the methods previously discussed.
- ✓ Make sure all your titles and text are correct.

INDEX

A non-fiction book printed by a traditional publisher will almost always have an index. It can be extremely useful for getting straight to the information you need within a book. The index is usually the last section.

An index will usually be formatted in columns across the page (two or three) with the term being referenced at the left margin of the column, sub-terms slightly indented and each term followed by a list of page numbers where it appears (sometimes a range of pages). Italics are quite often used in the formatting and emboldening is used for the most relevant page numbers.

Microsoft Word has an automatic Index Function whereby you have to mark the text you want to include and it creates the index for you, much like the Table of Contents Function. Unless you are experienced at creating an index (indexing is a recognised profession in its own right), I would suggest that this is the only way for you to reasonably create your own. The index must be the last thing you update, because any changes to the text could have a massive impact on the accuracy of your index. You have to be certain of the types of things people are likely to want to search for and you will have to make sure you don't miss out any instance in your index – you could, perhaps, use the Find Function for this.

eBook

An index is of little use in an eBook. Quite simply, this is because the book doesn't have page numbers. In order for it to be effective, it would have to be linked back to every indexed point in the text. When you consider how many of these there would be in a normal non-fiction book, I think you will see the enormity of this task. (Just take one of your writing manuals off the shelf and browse through the index to get an idea.)

I have never seen a non-fiction eBook with an index, although I have heard mention of books that do have them. With the search function available on most eReaders, it really isn't necessary. You won't be bucking the trend by leaving one out.

POD

If you are creating a POD non-fiction book, you really should have an index. Test out how to create one in a separate document (say the first couple of chapters of your book), before you do your final version, to iron out any issues with the process – it takes days to do, not just a couple of hours. I have included a short index in the print version of this book so you can see what can be achieved with Microsoft Word.

An index will usually start on a right-hand page.

Proofreading Checklist

✓ With an automatically generated index there shouldn't be any issues. However, I would still carefully check that all the entries are correct. You can do this in two ways. Firstly, by looking up all the entries that the index highlights and secondly, by finding all relevant instances of the term (other than simple mentions) in the text and then checking that they are listed in the index.

✓ Make sure that the entries are easy to read and check the spellings. If you have used highlighted text as the referenced item and the spelling is wrong, it is wrong in the text too. Otherwise, you will need to simply correct your index entry.

✓ Finally, ensure that the display works well on the page. Try to ensure that all the columns are the same length on the page, apart from the final one.

EBOOK FORMATTING SUMMARY

A RANDOM LIST OF FORMATTING TO AVOID WHEN SELF-PUBLISHING YOUR MANUSCRIPT TO AN EREADER PLATFORM

I've covered the general proofreading rules and talked a fair bit about the formatting and display of your eBook, but there are a number of specific things you should try to avoid when preparing a document for an eReader platform that might be perfectly acceptable in a printed book. These should be added to your proofreading tasks and are best carried out in your last round of on-screen proofreading. Some of them have been mentioned before, but I wanted to illustrate them here so that you could see the issues for yourself as you read. In the eBook version, these should be obvious on your screen. In the print version, I have tried to emulate the effects.

Can you guess what the first one is? No? I've given you a huge clue up there, at the beginning of this chapter. Never mind. The things you should try to avoid are:

Really Long Titles (in large font sizes)

If you use a very long title (like the title to this sub-section), depending on which size the reader displays the text at, it may span across several lines, possibly even taking up most of the screen if they're reading on their phone. And then there's the justification issue. This is not a good look for your book. Pare your titles down as much as possible during the editing process before you even get to the proofreading stage. For example, the title here could have been trimmed down to something like 'EBook formatting errors' or 'Don't do this in your eBook'.

Long-Strings-of-Hyphenated-Words-Simply-Because-It's-Cool

Once again, these can span over more than one line and create a very unbalanced visual experience for the reader (and that could make the meaning of what you are trying to say very unclear).

OneReallyLongWord/Another/PerhapsAnother

Long words with a slash between them can be a real problem when viewed on an eReader. A slash will stick the words together and you could end up with weird extra line spaces in your text, or words splitting without a hyphen, because of them. Use a word instead if you can – or, and – whichever is appropriate.

Dashes—With No Spaces Either Side

Once again, these can create a bad visual experience on the page because the lack of a space usually binds the words together, especially if you are using this type of dash with long words. If you add a space either side of the dash, the text can wrap normally – and to my eye is more visually pleasing anyway. Of course, there are places where this would be inappropriate, eg, at the end of a piece of interrupted speech or, as in this book, if you are using them to format readable bullets.

Really Tiny Font Sizes

It is very annoying for a reader to have to keep on changing the size of text to be able to flip between two or more books. Make sure your fonts are normal sizes (usually 10 or 12 pt).

Script Fonts or Excessive Italics

Apart from being really difficult to read in large amounts, you may find that the eBook conversion doesn't support the font you have chosen and converts it back to a basic font anyway.

Very Large Indents

Once again, these can create a strange visual experience for the reader. Don't do it.

Tabs to Create Indents

Tabs will not work for indenting your paragraphs properly when your manuscript is converted (and they don't really work anyway, to be honest). Use the Indent function and create a Style for your paragraphs instead.

Spacing to Create Indents

I don't mean to be unkind, but this kind of spacing shows no understanding of word processing at all.

If you want to create eBooks (or any type of book, for that matter), you really need to learn how to use a word processor properly.

Any forced spacing, using the spacebar, might create an uneven look to your manuscript when it is converted, especially if you hit too many, or too few, spaces.

Excessive Use of the Return Key

Generally, when trying to create extra space between paragraphs or headings, you should use the Paragraph Spacing function.

If you simply keep pressing return you might find that conversion gets rid of all of the returns and your text has no separating space at all. One return is usually enough, for anything more, use Paragraph Spacing. (I pressed three before this paragraph, by the way. It may, or may not, have worked for your eReader, if you have the eBook version.)

EBOOK FORMATTING CHECKLIST

I've gathered the main formatting elements you need to implement together here as a quick reference list. Now that you've read the rest of this book, you should understand them and their significance.

- Use a normal font. By that I mean something like Times New Roman or Arial (the normal Arial, not 'narrow' or 'black'). Many fancy fonts are not supported by eReaders and will convert back to the standard font. Even Arial isn't supported as standard.
- Use a normal font size – 10 or 12 point, preferably 12.
- Make sure the colour of your text is set to 'Automatic' and not 'Black'. It will appear as black, but specifying it as such doesn't work if a reader sets their device to read white text on black. They see nothing.
- Leave your body text as left-aligned – do not justify unless the platform specifies this. Justification is usually carried out by the conversion process.
- Format your body text as Normal Style in Microsoft Word. If you don't, conversion is unlikely to run smoothly.
- Format your headings using the Heading Styles in Microsoft Word, eg, Heading 1, Heading 2, etc. If you don't, you won't be able to use the Table of Contents Function and the conversion process may not recognise them as headings.
- Keep the font size of your headings at no more than 14 point (unless you have very short headings). Any larger and they may extend down half the reading screen.
- To change fonts to your preference, use the Modify Function for Styles and alter an existing Normal or Heading Style.
- Do not use end-of-line hyphenation in your text. Lines of text are reflowable depending on the size viewed and hyphenation won't work.

- Never include page numbers or headers and footers. EBooks do not need them and do not support them.
- If your book is very short, consider putting some of your front matter (such as Acknowledgements, About the Author) at the back of the book so that people downloading a sample, or using a Look Inside feature, will see enough of the text to gauge whether or not they want to buy the book.
- Make your Contents Page interactive (ie, clickable). If you don't do this, there is no point in having a contents page as there are no numbered pages in eBooks.
- Avoid the excessive use of page breaks (preferably only use them when a new chapter or story starts). White space in a print book is good, white space in an eBook is unnecessary.
- Ensure that you create an About the Author page with your bio and have clickable links to your website and other places where you can be reached or followed.
- Place a brief blurb about your other publications at the back of your book, with clickable links, if appropriate. If you decide to add a sample chapter, I would suggest that you make sure it is an absolute maximum of ten per cent of the text.
- Only create clickable links to books sold by the same retailer, eg, don't link to an iBookstore edition if you are publishing on Kindle. The retailers don't like it and will probably reject your book.
- Simplify your hyperlinks by linking them to text, ie, don't simply copy a website address and place it in your document unless it is a compact address.
- Don't place too many clickable links within your text. People may inadvertently click on them when changing the page and get annoyed.
- Use separators to indicate section or scene breaks.
- Don't use automatic bullets and numbering. Choose a simple bullet marker to define your list and let the text warp to the left-hand margin.
- Insert graphics using the Insert Picture function and ensure they are an appropriate size and dpi for the format.
- Before you convert the document, press the Update Table of Contents button one last time.

I'VE CONVERTED MY EBOOK FILE – NOW WHAT?

You've performed all your proofreading tasks on your manuscript. You've formatted the file perfectly. You've pressed that convert or upload button on your eBook platform and now you have a new file. Your eBook.

Take a deep breath – you're not finished yet.

You should have ended up with a beautiful file that reads well and flows perfectly.

Should is the operative word here.

Manuscript conversion does not always go perfectly, no matter how carefully you think you've formatted your file.

Use all of the reading formats available to you to check your file again before publishing (it won't necessarily display in the same way on a mobile phone as it does on an eReader) and concentrate on each of these points in separate passes. Most of them have already been mentioned in individual sections.

Don't worry, they won't take too long if you find no errors, but don't skimp on them. If you only check the first twenty-five per cent of your book, you can guarantee there will be an error at twenty-six per cent.

- Flick through and check that all your headings are in the correct format. If you find one that spans over three lines in normal eReader size, try and shorten it.
- Check your indents – if you used traditional novel format, make sure every first paragraph in a chapter or section is left-aligned rather than indented.
- Make sure your text is fully justified (straight down both sides).
- Test your book with white text on a black background. If your text is invisible, you haven't used the Automatic option when defining your font, you have specified black (which won't show up on black). Go back and reformat all your text to Automatic.
- Check all your hyperlinks (including your Table of Contents links). If something doesn't work, redo the link.
- Make sure you are able to 'Go To' the Table of Contents. If you can't, you haven't created that particular Bookmark correctly.
- Look at all your graphics – are they readable? If you enlarge them are they still readable or does the quality degrade? You may need to import them at a different dpi if this is the case.
- Check for any characters that aren't displaying correctly (eg, accents, maths symbols). If they aren't, you may have to omit them completely and find an alternative way of expressing what you want to say.
- Are there any strange or uneven line endings? Look at the text around where this happens. Could it be a hyphen or a slash that has caused this? See if you can use something different instead. If the only format

in which this happens is a mobile phone display, don't worry too much. The screen is so small that it would be difficult for it to display perfectly.

- Look at where the ten per cent mark falls in your document. This is likely to be where the Look Inside or sample will end. Is it enough for someone to decide whether they should buy your book? You may need to move your front and back matter around if it isn't.
- Finally, read through all the text again. There's bound to be something that slipped through.
- If you find any errors, upload a new file and check again.

Only when you've done all these checks and you're absolutely sure you cannot find any errors, should you press that publish button.

My Experience

I can't stress enough how important it is to make sure you flick through your entire book in all the formats available. I spent a whole morning doing this one task for this book (actually, I did it twice, but the second time only took an hour and a half). It is monotonous and boring, but you must keep alert – you'll be surprised by what you find.

Below, I have highlighted the problems I found in the online and downloadable Kindle previewers.

- I found a couple of paragraphs right near the end of the book where the line spacing seemed different from everything else in the Kindle Fire emulation – it had been fine on my PC app and my basic Kindle. I went to the paragraphs and re-assigned the Normal Style and they did change, almost imperceptibly, but it was enough to throw the formatting out.
- On the iPhone previewer I found that my first title, Introduction, wasn't formatted at all. I reassigned the style and put an extra return on the previous page (the Table of Contents). On re-uploading, this didn't entirely solve the problem, as on initial display it was still unformatted, but when scrolling back and forth between pages, it did display correctly (this was probably an emulation glitch).
- I found that, on the emulations for iPhone and iPad, my title styles didn't work in the same way as on other displays and devices – the font was not changed to Arial and the All Caps function was not implemented. After thinking about this for a while, I remembered that years ago, when I used an Apple Mac, it didn't have the Arial font – the equivalent was Helvetica. However, the titles were well differentiated in the way they did display, so I didn't change them. The thing

that it did highlight, though, was that the capitalisation of some of my titles (ones that had previously been All Caps) needed adjusting.

- I also found on the iPhone emulation that titles split over two pages didn't display properly on the second page. This might have been a problem with the emulation, but it wasn't something I could do anything about anyway.

- On the iPhone emulation I noticed that some of the spacing around titles seemed uneven. This may have been an emulation problem, but I went back to the document and redefined the paragraph spacing to try and ensure that this wouldn't happen.

- On the iPhone emulation I noticed that text is hyphenated by the system, but very badly. There was absolutely nothing I could do about this, but it was interesting to see. My favourite was the title Running Head(lines), which ended up as:

**Running Head(-
lines)**

***

Skimp on this stage of proofing at your peril.

SANDIE GILES

POD FORMATTING SUMMARY

A RANDOM LIST OF FORMATTING TO AVOID

The issues that mark a book as looking unprofessional in a print book are somewhat different to those for an eBook. That is mainly because it is much easier to look at a print book as a whole and see the inconsistencies and because eBooks are new and readers tend to forgive more with them.

Here are some of the things that you should avoid.

- Badly displayed front matter, eg, a Copyright Page not centred horizontally (and vertically).
- Chapters that start right at the top of the page.
- Chapters that run on from the previous page.
- A contents page with incorrect numbering.
- Page numbers on your title page.
- Uneven page lengths.
- Text that is too small to read easily.
- Widows and orphans.
- A non-customised book cover (ie, you have left it the same as your eBook and have not included information on the back page).
- Too many different fonts on a page.
- Gapping or squashed text where lines haven't been hyphenated.
- Inappropriately hyphenated words.
- Blurry (or unclear) graphics.
- Mislabelled graphics.
- Footnotes on the wrong page or incorrectly numbered.
- Badly split titles.
- Text wrapping around an image too closely.
- Inconsistent heading styles.
- Two spaces between sentences.
- Badly formatted bullet lists.
- Underlined hyperlinks still in the text.

POD CHECKLIST

Most of these things have been mentioned before, but they are gathered together here for convenience.

- Use a normal font like Times New Roman, Garamond or Arial for your main text.
- Use a normal font size – 10, 11 or 12 point.
- Make sure your body text is justified.
- Use end-of-line hyphenation so that the words are better spaced out on each line.
- Add page numbers and running headers.
- Create a table of contents with page numbers.
- White space is good in a print book. Space things out more so that they are well displayed.
- Ensure that all your chapters start on a right-hand page.
- Start your chapters about a third of the way down the page. Make the title styles more interesting. Consider using Drop Caps for the first letter of your chapter.
- Go through your book to remove all widows and orphans.
- Ensure that all your page lengths are the same, except at the end of a chapter.
- Choose a professional style of bullet list for any displayed text.
- Choose heading styles that are appropriate to your genre.
- Ensure that all your graphics are the appropriate dpi for the production process. Place them as close as possible to the mention in the text and number, if appropriate.
- Display your front matter and back matter evenly on the page.

I'VE GOT MY PROOF COPY BACK – NOW WHAT?

Checking a proof copy is similar to checking an eBook copy, but it may take you a bit longer as it's more difficult to look at all the pages. Once again, these things have all been mentioned in the individual sections previously.

- Before you do anything else, check all the page numbers. If they don't run in order, something has gone wrong with the printing. Contact the POD publisher for an explanation.
- Look at your cover. What is the printing like? Does it look sharp? Does it have impact? If it doesn't look like you expected, you may need to upload a new cover image. Check that the dpi is high enough according to the POD publisher's instructions.

- Make sure that your running headlines appear in each section (chapter). Check the text in each section (all the headlines in a section will be based on the same text so you only need to do it once for each).
- Look at the front matter. Is it displayed well on the page? Does it look like you expected it to? Is everything on the correct page (left or right)?
- Look at the chapter beginnings. Is the title far enough down the page? Is the title big enough? Has the drop cap worked? Is the first line of every chapter (or section) left-aligned?
- Do the chapter breaks work well? Is there enough white space to define them?
- Check your indents.
- Make sure all the text is justified.
- Is the back matter displayed well?
- Read through the entire text again. Are there any errors? If you find something and correct it, be careful that it doesn't change the formatting (end-of-line hyphenation, page endings, etc). If it pushes text over the page you will have to go through the whole document from that point on and make sure the formatting is still okay – try to avoid this if you can.
- Check the page lengths for evenness.
- Check the display of footnotes and endnotes is consistent.
- Check the quality of the printed graphics.
- If you have to change something major, you will need to order another proof copy and check that again. Don't be tempted to press publish without this – you may live to regret that decision if you do.

And finally, when you are sure everything is correct, press publish.

My Experience

Formatting for a POD book is very different to formatting for an eBook and, contrary to what you might think, takes a lot more time.

I created the print version of this book on Amazon's Createspace using one of their pre-set templates. The templates are great. They set out all the formatting for you and it's easy enough to change text styles on the page if you want to. However, there were some things which you could find confusing (I know I did to start with).

The first part of the template, ie, the front matter section, is formatted with the right-hand pages in the book as left-hand pages in the template. What I mean by this is, if you look at it with two pages side-by-side on the screen, then the right-hand pages are on the left. However, when you get to the main part of the book, the right-hand pages appear as they would in the book, on the right-hand side. The way you can easily tell this is by looking at how the margins display, ie, which side they are widest. The widest side is where the pages will be bound. This meant that, because I wanted my contents page to appear on a right-hand page, I had to make it start on a left-hand page. This is very difficult to get your head around when you're looking at it on the screen. Just accept it. When the book is converted everything will be okay as you will see in the online previewer.

This also caused me a problem with the transition from front matter to the main text, because I ended up with a completely blank page, front and back, between the end of the contents and my introduction, even though there was only one blank page in the source document. The only way to solve this was to remove the one blank page in my source document and cross my fingers that it would come out right during conversion. It did. The conversion clearly inserts a blank page (side) between the front matter and the main text to make the book work, so you mustn't have any blank pages there if you want to avoid the problem I had.

You can upload your file as many times as you want before confirming it, so don't worry about these things. Just play with your document until everything works.

Another issue I had was with the quality of my images. They needed to be 300 dpi and they weren't all that quality to start with. I had to do a little playing around with the images for it to work, but that wasn't too difficult. If you don't know what dpi your images are, you can right-click on the source file and look at the properties.

Creating the cover file was very fiddly. I wanted the image to be the same as on the eBook, but I had to completely recreate the image in order to do this. My issues, however, were more to do with my graphics abilities than anything else as the templates are well set out and easy to follow.

My biggest problem of all was not with getting the book into paperback format – it was creating the index. This is such a time-consuming task and it isn't something you can work on for hours on end because it sends your eyes and your brain into meltdown. I know my index isn't anywhere near perfect and I could've made it a lot more detailed, but that would've taken weeks to do (I'm not joking) and I'm confident that my contents page is detailed enough for this not to be absolutely necessary. If I revise the print version again in the future, I might tackle the index again.

So, be prepared to spend several days formatting your book file for print, especially if you have anything more complex than a very straightforward novel.

I'VE PRESSED PUBLISH – NOW WHAT?

Go to the website and check your listing very carefully.

- Is the thumbnail for your book good enough to entice the reader to buy? Ask other people to look at it and give their opinion.
- Proofread everything in your book listing – book title, author name, blurb, etc, again.
- Look at the sample or Look Inside. What do you see? Is it a perfect representation of the book? Can you see enough of the content?
- If you are publishing on a site that supports it, make sure you have created an Author Page and claimed your book (you might need to do this in each individual country where your book is being sold). Proofread carefully anything you put on your author page.
- When you're happy with everything – tell everyone about it!

If you do find an error after you've published (or someone picks up on an error in a review), it isn't a complete disaster. You can always upload a new file that will overwrite what was there before. Some people suggest that you put an inconspicuous code on your copyright page so that you can ensure the correct file is being offered to customers. I think this is a sensible idea.

SANDIE GILES

PROOFREADING ISN'T JUST FOR YOUR BOOK

As well as your book, there will be many other instances where you will need to ensure that your text is as near perfect as it can be. This is not an exhaustive list, but I hope it highlights how careful you will need to be from the moment you call yourself an author.

Once you have published your book, everything you write in the name of that pursuit, or otherwise, will be under scrutiny. Don't let anyone have cause to doubt your expertise.

YOUR BOOK BLURB

This is the text that goes on the retailer's website telling potential readers what your book is about.

Your blurb is one of the most important things you have to write apart from the book itself. You need to capture the essence of your book and give enough information about it to entice readers, but not so much that you give everything away.

Try to write it in the same style as you did your book and proofread it a hundred times if you need to (always print it out before you upload it) – this is the face of your book. It has to be perfect. Ask friends who are interested in the subject or genre if they would be interested in the book simply by reading the blurb. Look at the descriptions for other books in the same category as yours – does it hold up against them?

And remember, you can always change your blurb if you find it isn't working.

BLOG TOURS

If you arrange a blog tour to promote your book you are going to have a lot of extra text to write and submit to the blog hosts.

Although you won't be the person formatting the text, and to a large extent you will have to trust someone else to make it look good, you must make sure there are no errors in your text. Remember, a lot of the people who read these blogs are authors too and they tend to be more critical than a regular reader – even if they don't say it to your virtual face.

Always attach a short paragraph about yourself, a link to your book and an image of the cover that they can use.

PRESS RELEASES

You might be tempted to send out a Press Release to your local news-paper(s) – they are unlikely to print anything about your book if the press release is riddled with errors.

If you do create a press release, be sure to include your contact information. It is possible that the publication might want to interview you rather than just rehashing the content you send them.

You should also include:

- Your book details;
- The date of the press release;
- A few direct quotes from you that they can use (in third person);
- Brief information on plot or subject (this could be a copy of your blurb);
- If you have a few good review quotes, you might want to include them;
- Details of where people can buy the book;
- A list of your social media addresses.

Remember, if they want more information, they can contact you.

Print it out and check, check, check.

FORUM COMMENTS

Many people don't seem to think that the accuracy of their spelling and grammar is important when they comment on a writing forum. This couldn't be further from the truth. Even if they don't consciously do it, people make assumptions about you from what you write.

I don't actively participate in any forum, but I do read what is written in some. It is unlikely that I would ever buy a book by someone who could not string a simple sentence together correctly, even if it was in an informal context. Yes, everyone accepts that an odd typo will occur every now and then, but misspellings in every other word will do your image no good at all. And don't forget, many of these sites are easily accessible by readers as well.

Take your involvement seriously. You may well have had your book professionally edited and proofread (although, if you're reading this, I'm guessing not), but if you can't comment without making lots of errors, consider carefully whether or not you should.

OTHER SOCIAL MEDIA

Where are you? Facebook? Twitter? Google+? Blogger? Wordpress? Tumblr? Flickr? Author Central? There are hundreds of places you can be and comment on the internet.

Your comments might only be short sentence responses (or less than one hundred and forty characters), but if you make errors, the impression people will get, rightly or wrongly, is that you are slapdash with your writing.

Check and check again before you press send.

ARE WE FINISHED YET?

Well, yes and no.

You are now armed with many tips and techniques on how to perfect your manuscript. Don't think that you have to tackle each element individually as I have done in this book. Once you know what you are looking for, you can easily group together all the spelling, grammar and punctuation checks in one document pass. Likewise with the formatting checks.

Spend some time analysing the kind of errors you are more likely to make. Take a sample chapter of your book and make a chart of all the errors and see if there are any patterns or particular areas of concern. Spend extra time on those areas when proofreading, ensuring that you do as much as you can to eliminate them.

Remember that some of these techniques can be used on your electronic document before printing out, or while editing, and will only take a few minutes to implement. Others involve you doing a little research into grammar rules or making lists of words you misuse or misspell for reference – this can be done before you start proofreading and will only need to be done once. Don't skimp on these preliminary stages or you will make the latter stages more difficult.

Above all, make sure you allocate enough time to carry out your proof-reading properly and try to enjoy it rather than seeing it as a chore. If you go into it with a positive mindset, you will almost certainly finish with a better product.

AVOIDING ERRORS IN THE FIRST PLACE

What can you do to help avoid making errors in the first place? That's a difficult one.

You could try to learn the dictionary off by heart, or play an audio version of a grammar book in the background while you're asleep.

Okay, the serious answers now.

Learning to type properly will go a long way to help you avoid making typos and introducing extra spaces between words, etc. It is well worth the time investment and it will also make you less likely to suffer from typing-related aches and pains in the future – a real concern if you intend to make writing into a career.

Learning to use your word processor properly (using Styles, as mentioned many times previously, for example) will help you to avoid formatting errors. It might be an uphill struggle, but once you've learned it, you will be able to perfect the formatting of your documents in a fraction of the time. If you decide to do this by attending a course, make one hundred per cent sure that they cover the things you need to know before you cough up the money. Many of the functions you need to use are advanced, not basic.

Create crib sheets of things you need to look out for. Remember earlier I suggested keeping a list of the words that you commonly misspell beside you? Simply writing these words down will help to fix the correct spelling in your head (remember when you used to write stuff down when you were cramming for exams?).

Try to avoid working on your manuscript when you are tired, because you will be much more likely to type the wrong word or the wrong name. I know this is not always possible, especially if you have a full-time job to cope with as well as your writing, but if you do work into the early hours, expect to have a tougher proofreading job at the end of it.

And finally, the more familiar you become with the kind of things you need to look out for, the more conscious you will be of the errors as you make them. For those who are already touch typists, you will know that when you type the wrong letter, you often know that it is wrong and you're already backspacing to make the correction before you even realise it. The same is true of all the proofreading errors mentioned in this book. Being aware of them means they are more likely to jump out at you.

So, work hard at learning the craft of proofreading and look forward to the time when everything becomes clear.

PROOFREADING IS TOO DIFFICULT

I hear you. In fact, I'm pretty sure I told you how difficult it was when you started reading this book, but then anything done well is difficult. Proofreading is a skill and not everyone will be able to achieve a high enough skill level to effectively proofread their own writing.

If that is you, you really should employ the services of a professional proofreader. But how do you go about finding someone?

There are many people who advertise on the internet offering all types of book preparation services, including proofreading. The vast majority of these have sprung up in the past two or three years as a result of the ePublishing explosion. Trying to find someone competent and reasonably priced has become a minefield.

I would recommend that your starting point should be the professional organisation for editors and proofreaders within your country. The staff should be able to provide you with a list of properly qualified proofreaders who can be guaranteed to do a good job with your manuscript, but I would still always ask for references (ones that you get directly from their clients, not pre-prepared ones) and examples of their work. Some may even offer to proofread a number of pages or chapters for free before you commit.

If you would rather go on recommendations from your writing colleagues and contacts, then I would suggest that you also read book(s) that have been proofread by this person or organisation. What do you think of the job they did? Were there things they missed that stood out like a sore thumb to you? Would you be happy if such errors remained in your book after proofreading? (The answer to that last question is, of course, no.)

When it comes to using friends of friends to proofread for you, bear in mind that just because someone has an English degree, a good grasp of grammar and spelling, and is willing to do the job for a couple of bottles of wine, doesn't mean that they fully understand the conventions of proof-reading, the formatting conventions of ePublishing, or how to maintain your writing voice while making changes. What would happen, for example, if you sent them your manuscript electronically and it came back corrected for spelling and grammar errors, but the text was completely messed up in terms of formatting and no longer sounded like you? I don't suppose you'd be happy. Be absolutely sure of what you are getting.

Once you have decided which route to take, find out:

- How they proofread. Is it on paper or on screen?
- What they will provide you with when they finish? Will it be a hard copy with corrections marked that you will then have to transcribe, or an annotated word document where you will have to accept or decline all their corrections? Do you understand how to do this?
- Are they a native speaker of the form of English (British English, American English, etc) you use in your book?
- What elements of proofreading do they provide for the price?

Of course, you will need to sign a contract. I would suggest that the contract should, as a bare minimum, define:

- The total cost of the project and when they expect to be paid;
- Exactly what you require of the proofreader, ie, what they are checking for;
- The deadline by which the job is to be finished.

Finally, remember that even if you employ a professional, there is no absolute guarantee that your work will be error-free. All books contain errors that none of the people who checked them picked-up.

In order to help you with your search for a proofreader, a list of the professional organisations in the UK, the USA, Canada and Australia is provided in Appendix I.

I LOVE PROOFREADING – TELL ME MORE

That's fantastic news. I'm so glad that you've enjoyed learning about the process.

If you want to learn more about proofreading and maybe get a recognised qualification, I would recommend that you look for an accredited course in your own country. The organisations listed in Appendix I should be able to help you with this. The courses won't be cheap, but nothing worth doing ever is, is it?

Now, I don't want to dampen your enthusiasm, but I have a few words of advice.

When I signed up for my proofreading course I was full of enthusiasm. I had always taken pride in the documentation I produced at work and others I'd worked with often commented on the accuracy of my typing and how they rarely found a mistake when they checked it. I didn't exactly think the course was going to be easy, but I was filled with, what turned out to be, a false sense of confidence.

What I have outlined in this book might sound extremely thorough and very hard work to do properly, but it has been presented in a very informal way. A good proofreading course will be much more structured and demanding. There is also a lot that I haven't included (which isn't appropriate for the self-publishing market). I cannot stress strongly enough how difficult a good proofreading course is. Be prepared for that.

There will also be a few side effects that you may not have considered. You will start to look at pieces of text with a completely different focus. You will begin to get annoyed at how badly some books have been proofread because the errors will jump out at you. You will kick yourself for making even the tiniest mistake.

But, you will be safe in the knowledge that your books will be the best they can be when you proofread your own writing.

WHAT DO I REALLY THINK?

In the introductory chapter, I talked about whether or not it was a good idea to proofread your own book and I told you that I hadn't used any professional services to help me with this book. So, do I think this book is as good as it could be?

Well, I believe that this book could have been better if it had been professionally edited and proofread. That is true of any book. I'm sure there are plenty of things that I have missed because I am too close to the manuscript. Also, there is a point at which you have to stop going through the text or you would never publish.

However, if I had employed anyone to help, it wouldn't have been an example of what can be achieved on your own. Therefore, it wouldn't have fulfilled its objective – to inform you, the reader, if proofreading your own book is a viable proposition. I am happy that this book does, in the words of an old British advert, what it says on the tin.

I originally published this book in eBook only. When I was putting together the print version, I found things I wanted to change (mainly because, two months later, I wanted to phrase some things differently) and I changed those things in both versions. When you self-publish, books can evolve in this way, which I like.

Should you proofread your own book? I can't answer that question, but one thing I will say is this. How many of the deliberate errors in this book did you find? All of them? Most of them? None of them? It is much easier to see mistakes in a book that you didn't write. Take that into account when you make your decision.

If you decide to go ahead, I wish you good luck with your proofreading.

Oh, and do turn the page – I have something else to tell you.

... AND FINALLY

Do you remember at the beginning, I stated that, even in a book about proofreading, there might be errors in the text? You probably thought the ones that I highlighted as we went along were it in terms of deliberate mistakes. Well, I have to confess – there are more.

Five to be precise.

If you have been reading carefully, you might have noticed them. Well done if you did. I expected some people to be searching hard for them simply to catch me out (because if I were one of you, I would have). However, if you didn't see them, below are details of where the errors appear, although they won't be highlighted – you'll still have to find them.

Error 1 – Misspelled word (transposed letters) on page 108.

Error 2 – Missing full stop (on bullet point) on page 28.

Error 3 – Missing second bracket on page 64.

Error 4 – Inconsistent quotation marks (single and double) on page 84.

Error 5 – Repeated word on page 99 (the word, in case you can't find it, is 'relevant').

Any errors, other than the five above (and the ones highlighted as we went along), are unintentional.

Thank you for reading.

Sandie Giles

GLOSSARY

.pdf
A document that has been saved as an Adobe Acrobat file and can be read by using Adobe Reader, a free piece of software already installed on many computers. Many documents accessible on the internet are saved as .pdfs.

A5
A paper size that is half of A4 (UK standard letter size).

All Caps
Every letter in capitals.

Arabic Numerals
Traditional numbering system using 1, 2, 3, etc.

AutoCorrect Function
A function in Microsoft Word that will correct any misspellings, that have been set into the defaults, as you type.

Beta Reader
A person who will read through your book, usually for free, before it is published and gives feedback on it. It is often carried out as a reciprocal arrangement between two authors.

Block Style
All paragraphs fully justified, ie, straight down both left and right.

Blog Tour
A series of blog posts where the author guests on other websites to talk about their (upcoming) book.

Blurb
The description of your book that you upload onto retailer websites.

Bookmark
A marker, set in an electronic document, that can be used to jump to that point by means of a hyperlink.

Browser
Software by which you can access the internet on your computer.

Bulleted List
A typed list of items that is usually indented and uses a marker (bullet) to distinguish one list item from another.

Buzz Phrase
A phrase that becomes popular for a short time, usually in business.

Contents (Table of)
A table at the beginning of a book listing chapters and their page numbers or providing hyperlinks to chapters in an eBook.

Copyright
A legal right to the control of a book (or other musical or artistic work) with regards to publication and distribution. A work is in copyright as soon as it is produced and belongs to the person who created it, unless they sign it away by means of a contract (eg, to a publisher). It does not need to be registered anywhere, although some countries do provide the means to do this.

Decimal Point
The full stop between the number and any fractions of it, eg, 1.5. The decimal point may be seen or implied. In word processing and spreadsheets, it helps to make columns of numbers easier to read by lining them up to the decimal point.

Dedication
A short paragraph in a book that dedicates the work to someone special in the life of the author. It can sometimes be 'in memory of'.

Dialogue Tag

The attribution of dialogue to a specific person, eg, said Charles.

Disclaimer

A paragraph at the front of a book that states that the people, events and places in the book are from the author's imagination.

dpi (Dots Per Inch)

A technical specification for pictures that defines the quality of the image. A higher number of dots per inch gives a better quality picture.

Drop Caps

A large, often ornate, letter at the beginning of a chapter which drops down through two or three lines of text.

eBook

A book produced in a digital format that can only be read on a device such as a dedicated eReader, a mobile phone or a computer.

eBook Conversion

The process of reformatting your original manuscript (eg, your Microsoft Word document) into a format that can be read on a reading device, or app, in a reflowable format.

Editor

A person who checks a manuscript for accuracy, plot issues and suitability for the market.

Ellipsis

A series of three dots (...) to indicate a trailing off of speech or that some of a quote is missing.

Emboldened

Text that appears in bold.

End-of-Line Hyphenation

Hyphenation used at the ends of lines to split words between them, so that a squashed or gapped appearance in the text is avoided.

eReader

A device specifically for reading eBooks.

Footnotes and Endnotes

A series of notes inserted into the text to clarify information in the book. They can be located either at the end of a page (footnote) or the end of a chapter (endnote).

Forum (Writing)

A online community where authors can discuss the writing and publishing process.

Grammar Checker Software

Software that will scan your text on-screen and indicate where there may be errors.

Hanging Paragraph

A paragraph indent where the first line of the paragraph is at the margin and all subsequent lines are indented.

Headers and Footers

The spaces above and below your main text in your word processor where page numbers and running headlines can be placed.

House Style

The format used by a publisher for all of its books.

HTML

Hypertext markup language – a computer language used, amongst other things, for publishing on the web and in the production of electronic content for eReaders.

Hyperlink

A link that can be clicked on to take people to another place in your book, to a website or to start an eMail. Links are underlined and usually appear in a different colour to the text.

Indents

A function in word processing programmes that affects the first line of the paragraph by setting it in from the margin (or with hanging indents, sets the first line at the margin and the other lines in from the margin), thus avoiding having to use the tab key for this function. Indents should always be used instead of tabs when formatting text for ePublishing.

Index

A list of key words relating to topics covered within the book with relevant page numbers.

Initial Cap

The first letter of a word is capitalised.

ISBN

International Standard Book Number. A cataloguing system for books used worldwide. Each edition or format of a book requires a new number. Not all eBook retailers require ISBNs for eBooks and many POD retailers provide them for free.

Jargon

Language used in a particular profession, or by a specific group of people, that may not be understood by others.

Justified

Text that is straight down both sides, but that can still have first line indents.

KDP

The Kindle Direct Publishing platform that allows self-publishers to upload their own eBooks onto the Amazon website for sale.

Kerning

A process by which spaces between words and letters can be reduced, or increased, to improve the distribution of text on a page.

Leader Dots

The dots, usually found in a table of contents, that lead your eye from the title of a chapter to the corresponding page number.

Left-Aligned

Where the main text of a document is straight down the left-hand side of the page and ragged on the right. NB: First-line indented text can still be left-aligned.

Look Inside/Sample

A function on a retailer's website that allows you to read some of the book you are considering buying. This is usually about ten per cent of the total.

Lower Case

Letters that are not in capitals.

Non-Breaking Space

A non-breaking space will not allow the words or numbers it is between to separate at the end of a line. It is achieved, in Microsoft Word, by pressing Ctrl + Shift + Spacebar at the same time.

Page Break

A function in your word processor that allows you to force text to start on another page.

Paragraph spacing

A function in word processing that adds extra space every time you press return, so that you don't have to press return twice to achieve spacing between your paragraphs.

Press Release

A document sent to publications announcing (in this case) a new book.

Print-On-Demand (POD)

A publishing service whereby books are only printed after they have been ordered.

Proof Copy

A sample copy of your POD book used for checking that it is correct.

Proofreader

A person who checks a book for spelling, grammar, punctuation and formatting errors.

Publishing House

A company that accepts books for publishing and provides all the services to enable the production of the book. The publishing house pays the author by means of an advance (but not always) and royalties according to the success of the book once released. Often referred to as a traditional publisher.

Reflowable

A recently coined term to describe a format by which a reader can change the size of text on a reading device and have the line lengths and pagination of the text automatically re-adjust. It is similar to word wrap on a word processor.

Right-Aligned

Text that is straight down the right-hand side of the page and ragged on the left-hand side.

Roman Numerals

Letters, originally used by the Romans, to represent numbers, eg, i = 1, ii = 2.

Running Headline

Text that runs across the top of the page in a print book detailing the book title, author or chapter details.

Section Break

A format option that splits your document (in a similar way to a page break) and allows different headers, footers, margins, etc, within each section.

Self-Publishing

Publishing your own book without the help of a publishing house.

Show/Hide Function

A Microsoft Word toolbar option that allows you to see where spaces, paragraph returns and other hidden formatting elements are on the page.

Style Sheet

A written description of the format-ting and word choices that have been made for a particular book.

Styles Function

A function in Microsoft Word that helps you to create pre-defined styles of text and heading (eg, font, font size, alignment, emboldening, italics, colour, etc) that can be applied to your manuscript. Conversion software used for ePublishing works better when Styles have been used.

Superscript/Subscript

Text that is positioned above the line/below the line, eg, in footnote markers and chemical symbols.

Tab

A ruler setting in your word processor that enables you to display text across the page at defined intervals, but that does not work well with eBook formatting.

Text Speak

The language often used when sending a text to another person, characterised by the extreme abbreviation of words, sometimes using numbers to stand for a particular sound.

Text-to-Speech Software (TTS)

Software that will read the typed text on your screen out loud.

Touch Typist

A person who can type using all their fingers and thumbs on the correct keys without looking at the keyboard.

Transcription

Transferring written corrections into your electronic document.

Transpose

To inadvertently place letters or words in an incorrect order.

Typesetting

Converting a manuscript into print-ready format in traditional publishing.

Upper Case
Text that is typed in capital letters.

Widows and Orphans
The first line of a paragraph appearing at the bottom of a page (orphan) or the last line of a paragraph appearing at the top of a page (widow).

APPENDIX 1

PROFESSIONAL ORGANISATIONS

Listed below are a number of professional proofreading and editing organisations that provide lists of qualified professionals. If you are thinking of employing a proofreader to help prepare your manuscript, I would recommend that you start with one of these (or the equivalent in your country).

UK

Society for Editors and Proofreaders
http://www.sfep.org.uk/

US

Editorial Freelancers Association
http://www.the-efa.org/

Canada

Editors' Association of Canada
http://www.editors.ca/

Australia

Institute of Professional Editors
http://iped-editors.org/

APPENDIX 2

GRAMMAR BOOKS

This selection of grammar books is by no means exhaustive, they are simply ones that I have found useful, but they are a good starting point for your reference library. The information within them is presented in different styles, from formal to humorous. You should be able to find one that fits with your learning style.

New Hart's Rules: The Handbook of Style for Writers and Editors (Reference)
R M Ritter, Oxford University Press

This book covers publishing terms, layouts, punctuation (UK and US usage) and many other aspects of writing. The text is formal, but easy to read and understand and uses examples to clarify points.

Oxford A-Z of Grammar and Punctuation
John Seely, Oxford University Press

This is a formal grammar book that covers all aspects of grammar, with extensive examples of usage.

English Grammar for Dummies
Geraldine Woods, Wiley Publishing Inc
Geraldine Woods & Lesley J Ward, John Wiley & Sons Ltd (UK)

This book covers the complexities of English grammar in the easy-to-use and familiar 'Dummies' format and has UK and US editions.

Eats, Shoots and Leaves (: The Zero Tolerance Approach to Punctuation)
Lynne Truss, Gotham Books, Penguin Group

A light-hearted look at punctuation with a serious message and written by a former editor.

APPENDIX 3

USEFUL WEBSITES

Grammar Tips

Grammar Girl – Quick and Dirty Tips
http://grammar.quickanddirtytips.com/

Daily Writing Tips
http://www.dailywritingtips.com/

POD Publishers

Create Space (Amazon)
https://www.createspace.com/

Lulu (also provides some distribution services for eBooks)
http://www.lulu.com/

Lightning Source
http://www1.lightningsource.com/

eBook Publishers

KDP Kindle Direct Publishing (Amazon)
https://kdp.amazon.com/self-publishing/

Smashwords (also provides distribution services)
http://www.smashwords.com/

NOOK Press (formerly Pubit – Barnes & Noble)
https://www.nookpress.com/

iBookstore (Apple)
http://support.apple.com/kb/PH2808

Kobo http://www.kobobooks.com/companyinfo/authorsnpublishers.html

APPENDIX 4

RETAILER SELF-PUBLISHING GUIDES

These are free guides to publishing your eBooks on the Kindle and Smashwords platforms and will help to explain some of the terminology and technical aspects if you have not yet published your first book.

Building Your Book for Kindle
Kindle Direct Publishing

Building your Book for Kindle for Mac
Kindle Direct Publishing

Smashwords Style Guide – How to Format Your Ebook (Smashwords Guides)
Mark Coker, Smashwords

ABOUT THE AUTHOR

Sandie Giles is primarily a fiction writer. She has had short stories published in paying magazines, speculative fiction anthologies and on other digital platforms. She has also self-published some of her work. She uses several pen names when writing to avoid muddying the waters between genres and Sandie Giles is her chosen name for her non-fiction publications.

Before pursuing a writing career, she spent many years in office administration and secretarial work, in environments where accuracy was of the utmost importance. She originally learned to type on a manual typewriter. There was no backspace delete key or copy and paste and errors weren't easy to correct, so you tried your hardest not to make them in the first place. That mindset has accompanied her through the progression to electronic typewriters and DOS-based word processing systems, up to the current WYSIWYG displays and touch-of-a-button correction.

She has a professional proofreading qualification and, although she has not pursued this as a career, it has been an invaluable tool for her writing.

ALSO AVAILABLE BY THIS AUTHOR

MICROSOFT WORD FOR WRITERS: CREATE A KINDLE TEMPLATE IN EASY STAGES

Sandie Giles

A step-by-step guide to creating a reusable template for your Kindle books.

MICROSOFT WORD FOR WRITERS: HOW TO MAXIMISE YOUR EFFICIENCY

Sandie Giles

Tips and suggestions on how you can improve your efficiency as a writer when using Microsoft Word.

SANDIE GILES

INDEX

CPSIA information can be obtained
at www.ICGtesting.com
Printed in the USA
LVHW092244010321
680328LV00025B/254